K SCOT MILLER

Pot Life

Untold True Story

To the trailblazers of cannabis culture: Cheech and Chong, Snoop Dogg, Dave Chappelle, Seth Rogan, Willie Nelson, Bob Marley, Mike Tyson and many more that had the balls to say they LOVE weed!!
Thank you.

Contents

"When you smoke the herb, it reveals you to yourself."

-Bob Marley-

Prologue

Settled originally by Cubans and renowned for its cigar industries, Ybor City, Florida. Now a unique visitor destination with many charming stores and diners and an Old Havana welcome. It is full of visitors on weekends and a quiet bearable neighborhood during the week. A tad like New Orleans and touch like Key West, from downtown Tampa, catch a ride on the trolley and view a thriving community. Clusters of restaurants, pubs, and several museums are accessible if you roam around.

Once a music store in the party district of Ybor City, now a forward-thinking smoke shop, Hot Wax Glass Co. concentrates explicitly on the customer journey, thanks to the courage of current co-owners Justin and Kevin. Collectively they realize using some risks and thinking outside the box can have tremendous payoffs.

Strolling past the Hot Wax storefront, within a tall side windowpane, witness our local resident artisan *"Red"* in live action. Witness the strange fire blazing from a torch as he gently handles the fragile glass, barehanded. The Hot Wax display draws in large gatherings outside. Eventually, they come inside the store.

By 2017, they had opened many Hot Wax locations throughout Florida. Justin and Kevin have come a long way since becoming friends nearly twenty years ago. They ended up moving from New York to Florida and recreating themselves.

Unlikely partners, Kevin came from the mortgage industry and Justin in furniture retail. Hot Wax prides itself on its branded smoking accessory products and enjoys cultivating a tribe of like-minded souls who cherish music, comrades, family, and community. Developing from all walks of life, faiths, and perspectives, brought together by cannabis culture, hipster culture, and cool shit!

Pot Life. The tale of how Hot Wax Glass Co became what it is now. An absurd and wild personal memoir, a coming of age story of the personal growth and perspective of K Scot Miller, co-owner of Hot Wax Glass Co.

Join the journey!

1

In an Instant

I t is July in Florida, and the weather turns steamy. I first heard the term *swamp ass* when I moved to Tampa, and I do not think there is a better description that comes to mind than that. It is muggy. Moist. It is gross. Now, the mornings are still somewhat pleasant, but you better get up early if you want any of that. By ten a.m. the *swamp ass* previously mentioned has made its presence known and felt. Now that I am in my semi-retired mode, I will try to get a morning run a few days a week, no need to rush into the office because there is not much to do.

I look down at my phone and see a text from Justin, my business partner. I look, eight a.m. Nice and early, I ponder as I put the phone down on the table. Justin is heading into the office. I will meet him later after this run, I am about to undertake. I open the door and muster the strength to start my warm-up and ease into my pace. I feel refreshed and think about how great my business is going, and I am proud of myself. Karen and I have been at odds lately; basically, we are not getting along. I did not care about any of that, though. I finish

1

up my sweaty attempt at a jog and head to the shower. My t-shirt is soaking in sweat as I strut through the front door. I hear Karen announce from the other side of the house, "Kevin, I'm taking Dylan and Jacob to Publix; they want their cookies." This meant free cookies for kids at Publix. She always enjoys taking our children for a quick treat, and I am feeling fantastic today.

I catch my breath, finally. "Okay," I shout back, "I'm jumping in the shower." I smile as I think about my happy, glowing children receiving their delicious treats like the kid Charlie in the movie *Charlie and the Chocolate Factory*. "See you when you get back!" I finish declaring. The shower feels revitalizing in this crazy Florida heat. I lose track of time as I turn the water knobs off and look around. Shit, I forgot to grab a towel. I run naked on my toes to the other side of the house to grab a fresh bath towel out of the laundry room. There are wet footprints and small puddles all over the tile. I will piss off Karen; I snicker silently. I take a deep sniff of the warm fresh laundry before shivering and wrapping up in pure, warm goodness. I try calling my business partners but get no response. Strange. Suddenly, a knock at the door.

Thump, thump, thump!

I jump up straight, and my head whips around to look at the door. Jesus! I clutch my heart and catch my breath. It is perhaps just another door-to-door salesman that has been crushing my neighborhood lately. These people are relentless, I theorize. I let out a deep sigh and...

THUMP! THUMP!

How annoying. I walk to the front door and get a peek through the front window. I draw back the sheer, lightweight curtains. Scanning the premise like a familiar book read a

2

hundred times, my eyes dart. The car is in the driveway, nothing unusual as far as I can tell. Who is this, and what the hell do they want, I wonder?

THUMP! THUMP! THUMP!

I make my way slowly, tiptoeing, heart-pounding, to the front door that has a small window; I look through. I lean in and peek through the small window, and a guy with a beard presses his head on the glass and shouts, "Open the door now, Kevin!" he commands.

Sputtering and stumbling over my words, I shrug. I shake my head, saying, "What, who are you? I…" instinctively, in a nanosecond, I know who they are. A rush of thoughts about the past few months floods my mind. Fuck. I am in deep shit.

"This is Sergeant Miller from the United States Marshal's office. Open the door, or we are kicking it down!" The bearded guy orders.

I jump back, look down at my wet body, and mutter, "Can I get dressed first?"

The guy enormously and firmly states, "Kevin, open the door now, or we're coming in." I reach out and hesitate to turn the knob, and just as I twist the lock, they hastily push in and snap me up. It is all a blur; I could not believe this is happening. Like the television show *Cops*, I am here, and this is happening. In an instant, life can change forever.

2

Winifred's Party

We are heading back to Grandma Winifred's party down the block from my childhood home near the Cove. It is a breezy summer night in West Islip, New York. Our parents have given us strict orders to 'leave for reinforcements' for the bar and come back briskly. My brother Geoff and I are on a mission. They instruct us to grab two bottles of Stoli vodka, one bottle of Bombay Sapphire gin, and Seven-Up.

We pick up the pace and race toward the house. The breeze feels refreshing, gusting gently off the Great South Bay. The moon reflects off the inlet water because of the high tide and gives just enough light to make our way in the darkness quickly over the lawn. We run toward the back of the house, passing the in-ground pool and through the sliding glass doors. Geoff is a few years older than me, and this time he beats me to the target.

"I still can't believe it, Kevin," Geoff says as he dances around and points at me with seemingly endless energy. "I'm going to B.C.! Do you know what this means!?" Geoff is drumming on the counter with his hands like some rock star drummer and has a huge wide grin on his face. I am feeling somewhat bitter.

"Yeah, you got in," I say flatly from the kitchen door. "Good for you," I fume. Rolling my eyes warily, I know B.C. means Boston College for Geoff, and I do not want to hear it. I want to have fun and do not want to think I still have High school to endure, summer employment to land, and I did not even have a girlfriend yet.

"Hell, yeah, good for me," he yells back in excitement. "I can finally get out of here, away from mom and dad… and you. I can start a whole new life in Boston." He swings his arms wide, chuckles, and skips around while heading toward the door to go back to the party. I did not say a thing and just kept on walking, but I am deep in contemplation. I imagine starting a new life away from mom and dad. How refreshing and exciting that could be, I muse. I slowly smile as I get caught in a moment of ideas. Geoff keeps on gabbing, but I do not hear a single word.

"So, what about you?" He yells out as we retrace our steps back to Winifred's. "Where do you want to go to school, do you have any idea, what are your grades, even like?" He inquires.

So many questions. "My grades are fine," I snap. "I'm working on them, and I don't know," I growl. With every word that Geoff speaks, my smile dissipates.

"You better; it's difficult to get into an excellent school. You better have other shit going on too, like extracurriculars, or you have no chance," Geoff nags.

I just want to get back to the party, and he is obnoxiously continuing. I am barely listening and get caught up in my own ideas about things. I am not sure why I am bitter about Geoff going to college. I suppose I feel like it will take so much time to get there, and I wonder how I can get noticed by people and especially noticed by the right girl. I am just a kid, and I do not want to concern myself with these things yet.

"You're going to end up at some crappy SUNY school… or maybe SCCC." He yells out condescendingly.

"SCCC, what's that?" I question with a confused look on my face.

"Suffolk County Community College!" he shouts. He laughs as if I should know his acronym, and he puts his bottle down on the kitchen counter. Walking away into the crowd, he is still laughing at his joke as I wonder if the trick is funny. Whatever, I roll my eyes and spin around, shrugging off my annoyances.

I make my way up to the back door at grandma's house and bounce in through the kitchen and down the hall looking for my mother. I find my mom socializing, having drinks, and cackling with the ladies about local rumors and hearsays. Dressed for the occasion, my mother is radiant. I hold up the two bottles of Stoli vodka, like holding the spoils of a siege. She smiles and points towards the back of the house and insists.

"Please give them to the bartender and then go get something to eat, okay, thank you, Kevin." She turns and continues her conversation with the ladies and never misses a beat. I feel as though my mom is enjoying the company and relaxing atmosphere. She looks happy, and my parents do so much for me. They work so hard for everything they have. They are good people and have a healthy relationship and marriage. High school sweethearts, both voted best looking. My dad was the student government president in high school. He played soccer, baseball and was captain of the basketball team. A straight-A student and graduate of the Wharton School of Business at the University of Pennsylvania. A tough act to follow. I proudly conclude that my parents genuinely exemplify that good old hard work pays off. Top of my list today is a smile on mom's face, along with finding Winifred down at the beach.

"Okay, I will, thanks, mom," I attest as I make my way through the crowd to my destination—the bartender.

It is another fancy affair at Grandma Winifred's home on the beach. Mostly an older crowd, stuffy, nicely dressed, and a faint smell of cigar wafting in the air. You must admire all my grandmother's distinguished friends, fashion style, and characteristics. They all have matching red, white, and blue outfits and tinkly accessories with tiny American flags everywhere. American flag toothpicks adorn the hors d'oeuvres. You know the type.

I finally get the bartender's attention from the other side of the wooden bar after repeatedly waving. Still, his focus is on the thirsty patrons, and then he gives me a thumbs up. I hand him the bottles, and in exchange, he hands me a Coke can.

"Here you go, kid, now go grab some food from the kitchen, thank you!" He exclaims. I make my way towards the back and outside for some fresh air. I stroll out the back door and immediately get hit with a salty breeze from the Great South Bay. I take a deep breath and then weave through the crowd down to the beach. I run down and bury my feet in the warm sand as I crack open the Coke can and look around. There is no one within thirty years of my age besides Geoff, I determine.

Out of the corner of my eye, I glimpse the most graceful person I know, my grandmother coming towards me as she talks to some guests. "Oh, Kevy, dear, how are you, mwah," she grins and plants a kiss on my cheek. I absolutely adore her British accent. She goes on, gushing, "Oh, my goodness, will

7

you look at you, you know, I think you get more handsome every time I see you," practically singing her words. I roll my eyes, but she continues, "It's true." She beams, "so handsome and tall, you're getting so tall." She looks closely at my hair, long in the back, and says, "oh dear, you may need a haircut." My hair has grown bushy on top.

"Thanks," I say, shyly giving her a big warm hug. Secretly, I love it when Winifred fawns on me during these gatherings. Suddenly, we hear the neighbor shout.

"Good news, good news, congratulations with college, Geoffrey, well done." Grandma Winifred smiles and waves at them; we watch Geoff shake hands, exchange hugs, and warm pats on the back with friends.

"I guess Geoff is spreading the news about getting into college," I complain, somewhat disappointedly to grandma. I look down, thinking about how my grades have slipped. I knew if anyone could understand my plight and struggle, it is Grandma Winifred.

Winifred responds, "Oh, yes, about Geoffrey getting into college." She conspicuously clears her throat, so I will pay attention. "So how are you doing in school, doing well?" she quarries as she raises her chin ever so slightly.

"Not really, my grades are not that good," I state, actually.

Winifred tilts her head, lifts one eyebrow, and looks straight through me. "Yes, well, my grades were not that good either; I hated school; it is just awful," she admits. With dad graduating from Wharton Business School and Uncle Bob being a successful entrepreneur, education is the top priority for Grandma Winifred. I am wrong.

Winifred interjects, "I left England when I was fourteen, and that was it for grade school and me; when I got to New York,

8

it was all about living life and finding your own path; grade school was not the path for me." She pauses for a moment before speaking again, leans in, and begs, "Kevy, dear, could you do me a big favor?"

"Okay," I say enthusiastically. I would do anything for my grandma Winifred, she is the best, and I love her.

"Kevy, I'm trusting you with my life on this one, dear," she says with a little wink. The suspense is killing me; I shake my head and shrug, wondering what she could want or need. She leans into my ear and quietly asserts, "I need you to head straight to the bar and have Barry the bartender get me a fresh vodka, no ice, and then bring it back to me at once. Can you do that for me, love?"

I laugh and agree, jump up, and start bouncing toward the bar to get her drink. I am reviewing my conversation with Winifred, enjoying my walk across the beach by many cheerful faces. In what seems like a snap, I appear at the bar, order grandmas drink and receive it in moments. It smells so potent, like rubbing alcohol and lemons. Gross, how can they drink this potion? I cringe outwardly.

I step out onto the beach to head back to Winifred and get hit with a powerful gust in my face. It whips my polo shirt and dirty blonde hair carelessly. We may not have fireworks in this weather. I make my way through the crowd to find Winifred, hand over the drink, and then head around the side of the house so I can avoid the happy-go-lucky partygoers. I do not feel very talkative, or maybe I just want some peace. The property is expansive, and like the familiar back of my hand, I skate through the layout. I slip through the side gate, around some large bushes, and then to the garage.

Suddenly, like a whirling dervish, the breeze whips up, my

nose detects a faint bouquet. The smell is pungent, but sweet. A little spicy maybe... with a hint of mint, I wonder? The strange thing is that the scent felt intimate, like I had smelled it a million times before, yet I did not know how to think about this. I am utterly confused and excited all at the same time. I need to go in quest of that smell, and in an instant, I notice a young man and woman huddling together, both wearing collared, pressed, white, button-up shirts.

I stop in my tracks and back up behind the bushes. I assume these individuals work with the valet service. What were they doing? Undoubtedly, they were giggling about something, I think. Meshed in close together, but they are not kissing. Huddling and passing something back and forth between their fingers, I squint to catch a glimpse, and then I spot a small glowing red ember, burning. My crusade is complete. I have discovered the source of the strange new fragrance. Is it a weird cigarette or... something?

Then poof, an enormous cloud of smoke billows in front of them, they cough loudly and uncontrollably. Hysterically laughing and hugging each other, they go on smoking and giggling quietly under their breath, as if people may hear them whispering. Still, there is not a single person anywhere nearby. Abruptly, they both jump as if they hear a noise, split apart in a panic, and disappear into thin air, gone! What happened, I wonder? This is so weird yet interesting, I determine.

3

The Summer Job

A quarter-mile from the Atlantic Ocean, overlooking the Fire Island inlet, is an oceanfront restaurant and sprawling nightclub; *The Oak Beach Inn,* or as we call it, *the OBI. Birthplace of the world-famous drink known as the Long Island Iced Tea. Invented in 1972, a bartender at the Oak Beach Inn, Robert "Rosebud" Butt, claims to have created the legendary cocktail beverage as a contest entry to make a new drink type. It was a tremendous success.*

Approaching *the Oak Beach Inn* overlooking the water, I see an L-shaped bar and deck with signs hanging on the side. It is windy near the water, and the movement of the large red letters and bold print blows up and flaps on the wood; the sign reads *Oak Beach Inn Water Toys-Jet Ski Rentals.* Parking is scattering out on Oak Beach's two-lane street, fueling anger in the small community. With summer here in July, people were spilling in by land and sea, sometimes boasting up to fifteen hundred young people at a time.

Self-made millionaire Bob, the owner of *the Oak Beach Inn,* is my uncle. Claiming to have spent millions of his own money to fight local and state government, many consider him to be an extremist, idealist, or even a weirdo. Arrested and criticized by locals, they either love him or hate him. My uncle Bob spends upwards of $25,000 a week in ads to urge the community to leave New York state. He takes out radio ads, whistle-blows, and calls out politicians. Still, some think it is just a gimmick for the ever-increasing overcrowding at *The Oak Beach Inn*. One campaign slogan proclaims *Slaves to the 9-5: "Move Out of New York State Before It's Too Late"* pasted on the side a hearse automobile rolling down Long Island Expressway. I hear so many stories about Uncle Bob. What a fascinating individual, I contemplate.

I need a car, I need to spend cash, I need a job. Dad already firmly states he is not helping me if I do not get my grades up. No passing grades, no car, period. Today my dad is taking me to *the OBI* for the first time to get my first job. We pull up to *the Oak Beach Inn* parking lot, there are hardly any spots, but we spot someone leaving and pull in. He puts the car in park and turns his face toward mine.

"Let us go find Barbara Jane, " he asserts and opens the door to get out. I follow and stagger behind. Just before going inside the back door to the kitchen and bar, he takes me by the shoulders. He looks down at me directly in my eyes, which could only mean that he really means business.

"Remember what I said before when we see Barbara Jane, shake her hand and make eye contact; she's a tough one, so just be polite," he repeats. Dad asks some workers to determine Barbara Jane's location when a bartender volunteers to help.

"Barbara Jane is in the office," he states while gently placing two glasses down on the bar top, grinning. "I can go get her," he insists. Short in stature and fit, maybe young, I think. He is one of those buff or meathead types, I conclude. As he walks away, I notice how dark and moist it feels inside the restaurant's bar area. The slight smell of cigarettes and alcohol lingers. I hear muffled voices, shuffling feet, and staff members are yelling in the back kitchen. Dad speaks up to thank the guy, and leaning in, he continues instructing me.

"When Barbara Jane comes, I will introduce you, and then I'll head to the car, come out when you're done; okay, here she comes." Barbara Jane is tall, maybe around six feet. She wears a Hawaiian shirt tucked into khaki shorts, and her hair is in a long ponytail. She is confident and energetic.

"Hey, Barbara Jane, how are you?" my dad inquires, smiling; he reaches out to shake her hand firmly, as he has a thousand times before. Closing real estate deals in West Islip with my mother, he has the handshake down pat, and this seems like a closed deal for me, a job at the hottest spot on the east coast, *The Oak Beach Inn.*

"Hey, Geoff, I'm great, how about you?" she wonders, shaking my dad's hand back with equal enthusiasm. Looking down at me and hesitating, she exclaims, "… and this must be Kevin, how are you doing, Kevin?"

I stand tall and answer, "I'm doing good; it's nice to meet you." Her eyes distract and dart toward the hustle and bustle of workers and staff, but she focuses back.

"So, I hear you are looking for a job," she casually guesses.

"Yes, Ma'am," I respond. I am convinced that I have the job, and I am so pumped.

She smiles and puts her hand on her chin, looks me up and down, questioning, "so, you're fifteen, I can start you out at the deli and see how that goes, what do you think?"

I glance behind my back; dad was walking out to the car as

promised. "Okay, I can be a bar back, too," I implore with a manipulative smirk.

Barbara Jane snaps back with a half-smile and quips, "Yeah, Kevin, let us not get ahead of ourselves; I do not think you're ready for that yet. I just want you to know that your uncle is notorious for firing people, so you will have to be on your best behavior… if you know what I mean."

"Okay, I will," I agree. I know my uncle. He is tough but fair, at least with me. "So, when can I start?" I ask politely.

"How about next Saturday morning?" she replies. "It'll be nine a.m. for deli setup; get here early to make a good impression," she advises and winks. I agree and shake her hand again, then turn to leave. A few steps from the door, Barbara Jane shouts toward me. "Alright, I will see you Saturday morning, and don't forget to bring your best behavior. I'd hate to see you get fired before you even start," she giggles. I can hear her chuckling to herself as I turn to make my way outside to meet my dad and tell him what happened.

Sweet, I got the job, I consider. Dad will be proud of me and maybe lighten up on me about the school grades. This job is going to be great; I might meet a girl, too. I smile and somewhat skip my way outside the back door. I make my way through some patrons as I am leaving to go home. I determine that this is a new start, a unique experience, I imagine. I proudly get in the car and start chuckling out loud.

"That was fast," dad marvels. He has been waiting for me in the car patiently. "So, how did it go," he giggles with a knowing look.

"I think I got fired already," I grin with a joking look on my face.

"What?!"

14

"Just kidding," I laugh and shake my head. "I start next Saturday morning at the deli," I announce. My dad pats my knee with firm force and proudly says, "There you go, Kev!" He beams with pride. "Your first job, that's great, there you go, so how do you feel working-man, do you feel responsible?"

"Yeah, dad, like a grown-up," I answer. I know that I will meet friends, girls, and people who will recognize me at *the Oak Beach Inn*. My uncle Bob is insanely popular, and *the OBI* is THE place to be anywhere on the entire east coast. This is going to be one hell of a summer.

My dad is laughing as he is pulling the car out of the parking spot; looking around, he looks back at me for a paused moment and says with a smile, "Good, now you can start saving for your first car. I'm serious; I will not help you get a car if you don't get your grades up, alright?"

I respond meekly, saying, "Yeah, dad, I know." The thought of school makes me cringe. For many, high school is an enjoyable experience with fond memories of homecomings and football games, school athletics, and high school parties. That is not the case for me at all. I am feeling like I do not fit the image my father had envisioned for my life. I cannot think about anything besides this new job at *the Oak Beach Inn* and being seen for once. People know my uncle and dad, and they respect them in the business world. It does not hurt to be part of this family, I confidently contemplate.

"Damn right, you'll get your grades up!" Dad verifies. I am feeling excited to tell mom the kick-ass news about the job. I wonder how I will pull off passing grades in school and have a radical, excellent social life. Daydreaming out the car window as we drive away, I fantasize about next Saturday at *the OBI*.

4

It Ends Before It Begins

A familiar piano synthesizer and drum beat thumps, and the familiar song lyrics play. *"There's a girl that's been on my miiind. All the tiiime... Su... sus.. sudio... oowhoahh..."* It is Phil Collins *"Sussudio"* playing on the radio, and my mom is singing out loud. She has gracefully volunteered to drive me to work. We must have been going 60 mph down the Robert Moses Causeway to go to *the Oak Beach Inn*; like the dark knight in a black bat-mobile, we fly down the highway in my mom's '84 Corvette. The buttery, camel leather interior practically hugs me as I slide into the seat. I love this car.

"Just be polite, pay attention to what people are saying and try to smile more," mom suggests. "Try to remember that whenever you are in a new place and meeting new people, attempt to introduce yourself to everyone," she adds.

I nod and say nothing. I am nervous when we arrive and give my mom a flimsy half-hug inside the car as I say goodbye. Sliding out of the seat and shutting the car door, I wave. The ramp leading to the deli seems longer than I remember, and I am uneasy. Still, somehow each inevitable step makes me feel like I am on my way to adulthood.

That day at *the OBI* delicatessen turns into many more long summer days. I could not make out much of the activity that has been happening in the club, just on the other side of the expansive building. I can see the bar in the building's front, but I am missing out on the action, I conclude. There is an upstairs karaoke lounge that looks like a 747 airplane. Rows of actual airplane seats line the sides of the room; it is wicked—the smell of fresh pizza and barbecue from the grill waft in, my stomach growls.

The crowd clears as a bar back whizzes past. I glimpse the enormous stage where live music plays almost nightly, and girls dance all night long until 4 a.m. sometimes. This place is a pleasure island, my paradise on earth. I have been mustering my courage for a few weeks to explore past my small square of deli restaurant space. So, I venture out onto the deck outside. Just as I step out on the wooden deck floor, I see a girl bungee jumping almost directly above my head.

"Three, two, one. Go, go, go," two men on top of a crane yell. I can hear them counting. High above, they seem to dangle freely. With a confident release, the girl leans out and shrieks. Dropping with such speed, she hollers as the rubber bungee cord stretches taut and springs back up as she continues to yell. Down she goes, upside down, and when the tension in the band reaches its max, the sheer force of gravity almost entirely takes her top off; bare-breasted, she flings back up.

Holy shit. I am in shock and laughing from the feeling of exhilaration the experience has given me at this moment. I try to keep quiet and to appear busy. Keep looking busy, I think silently, fearing reprimand from Barbara Jane. As my

17

workday concludes, it gets louder, and people act a little crazier. I theorize that life might be more enjoyable if I have time to work a night shift or mid-shift. So, I secretly plan.

Mom's 'Vette glistens and growls as it pulls up in front of *the OBI*. I am finishing my shift, and she drives me home most of the time. I proudly bounce over to the car and slink in the seat. I am ready and prepared to get my way with my mother.

"Hi, mom, Barbara Jane asked if I could help and stay late next Sunday; they need me to run the afternoon pizza station after my morning shift is over, is that okay?"

"That's a ten-hour shift," mom concludes. "I thought you said your feet hurt you after just a few hours, and now you're okay with ten hours on your feet?" she challenges gently.

"Yeah. I can handle it," I pipe with confidence.

With an innocent smile, she agrees, "All right, if you say so, just make sure you eat enough food and drink plenty of water. That's a long day, kiddo."

"I will; it's a deal," I concur. Where there is a will, there is a way. Changing the subject of conversation, I hint, "Are you making mama's meatballs tonight? I'm starving."

Mom laughs and nods her head and confirms, "Yeah, I guess I can; we're going to need to beef you up a bit for these long shifts, working man." We both laugh, but I sink in my seat a little; I look out the window at the Great South Bay as we drive over the Robert Moses Causeway. If I get busted, I am in trouble, like big-time trouble.

One week later, I am back at *the OBI*, I arrive early and start my deli prep duties, and I am finally free to roam. I head straight for the back of the bar and see Pat, the bar back. I walk toward him confidently and state, "I am told I'm bar backing until seven; what can I do to help?"

Pat enthusiastically suggests, "Just grab one of these bins and walk around looking for empty bottles and cups, fill them up and bring them to the kitchen and separate them. Check-in with the bartenders occasionally to see if they need anything and just stay busy. Do not let Barbara Jane see you slacking, or she will crush you. Like for real."

"Okay, okay, I'll watch out for her," I say confidently. I need to watch out for her, anyway; if she sees me, I will probably get in trouble, but I have not seen her in hours, so I hope she has left for the day.

The band is cranking rock music in the live music area, and they pack the floor. The plan is to blend in and look like I am busy. Most couples were making out in corners or out on the deck, and singles were on the prowl. A group of people slam shots at the bar and scream out unidentifiable words. It is all new and exciting to me.

I keep moving and make my way all the way outside to the end of the dock. It is a long stroll out, and it is warm outside. The inlet water lapped the wood-side of the pier. I walk around the other part of the ramp, still filling up a bucket bin with empty bottles and cups; I appear as if I have reason to be where I am not permitted.

I told mom my shift is nine to seven; I remember. The clock behind the bar reads 6:45. I need to leave. I turn around, and a girl is standing directly in front of me.

"My friend thinks you're cute," she flatters. Pointing toward her friend, she says, "She's a little shy, though. Do you want to meet her? She's right over there." I glance over at the girl. Cute brunette, not much older than me, I judge. I determine that fake IDs must be simple for girls to get these days; they can get in the really dope places that are admittance eighteen to twenty-one years of age and over. And they can buy drinks at the bar. Slurring her words a bit and smiling wide, she giggles with rosy cheeks.

She gushes, "I'm Lisa, I've seen you here before, and I told my friend here that I thought you were cute twice, and she totally took off and went over to you. I didn't ask her to, or anything." She is hella cute, I analyze.

"I'm Kevin. Nice to meet you," I greet with a shy smile.

Lisa grabs my hand and starts laughing and bouncing around. "Let's go dance, Kevin, show me what you got!" she giggles. With a gentle pull, I willingly follow as Lisa pulls me. Every few seconds, as we run around the outdoor deck and back inside the club, she looks back and smiles. All the way out to the middle of the dance floor, she pulls and turns toward me and starts dancing. *Take Your Time (Do it right) by the SOS band* plays over the speakers.

"Let's do it!" Lisa yells. "Kevin, I love this song!" Lisa shimmies close to me and starts swaying back and forth, shaking her hips. "Show me something, Kevin," she provokes. The disco dance floor is so crowded with dancers, energy, and excitement that there is not much room for me to worry about looking like a fool. I follow her lead and then move in close. We almost wholly stop dancing as our lips come so close to kissing. The crowd is lit, bouncing all around us and having the time of their life. Like a moment in time, frozen. Maybe this is what heaven is like. Entirely lost in a moment of bliss, I do not even realize the time as we kiss. Suddenly, a firm grip on my arm slings me straight out of my ecstasy moment and back into my boring reality.

"What the hell are you doing," Barbara Jane shouts. "Oh my god, it's almost eight o'clock, didn't you get off at four? Why are you here, Kevin? What the hell?"

I quickly respond, "I'm sorry, my mom is going to be late, so I tried to help the bar back out while I waited. Some girl grabbed me and dragged me on the dance floor. I'm sorry."

Barbara Jane huffs, "Just stay here, it doesn't matter how it happened, but I need to find your uncle Bob right now." She just freaks out and leaves, looking for my uncle. Still carrying his bucket bin, Pat brushes past me. He gives me a look, I read his eyes, and I know he wants to say you are a dumbass idiot without words. I shrug as he shuffles toward the kitchen dishwasher, and I sit for ten minutes until Barbara Jane returns.

"I spoke with Bob, and it's as I thought. I'm firing you, Kevin, stupid crap you just pulled." She shrugs and walks away.

"Really?" I question. "Fired?"

She spins back abruptly and says, "Uh, yeah, Kevin, I told you your Uncle Bob doesn't mess around, now go grab your stuff and go home." I grudgingly leave and pick up my bag from behind the deli and walk to the front exit, and that is when I see Uncle Bob.

"Hey buddy, I heard about what happened. Not good, not good. I hope your mom and dad don't get too upset," declares Uncle Bob.

I quickly apologize, "I'm sorry, Uncle Bob, because of my mom's delayed arrival, and I just got caught up with this girl, and… I screwed up."

"Yes, you did, and that's why you have to pay for it," responds Uncle Bob. "You're fired, and now I must listen to your parents yell at me too, not what I feel like dealing with. Have a wonderful summer, Kevin. Come back next May, and we can talk," Uncle Bob mutters as he walks away.

Bogus! Why did Uncle Bob spaz on me? I am so crushed

by getting fired from *the OBI*. I have lied to mom, and I must tell both my parents I am fired from my job and how embarrassing. I pivot from an unbelievable high to a crushing blow of disappointment in a matter of moments. This night is the first and last opportunity to experience behind *the OBI* scenes, and I blew it until next year. Sadly, it is over before it even begins. I silently pray I get another chance with Lisa.

5

The First Time

For the rest of the summer, I work as a busboy at Captain Bill's restaurant in Bayshore. I am lucky to get a job at all, I suppose, and I end up making a few friends, which I enjoy. Nothing like *the Oak Beach Inn* experience and I cannot wait until May next year to go back to paradise on earth, it seems. The most excellent existence I can dream of.

Unfortunately, with the coming of fall, school begins. I feel like I am a loser. I am friends with all the cool kids, and I am accepted, but deep down, when I think about it, I feel like they do not genuinely like me at all. I make two new sorts of acquaintances in school, gravitating to the troublemakers.

Mr. Smith, my English teacher, is well-liked and always has a few moments of laughter during each class; on this day, Mr. Smith has gone out the night before, or he was up late doing something. He starts with his typical high energy entrance into the room. Marching through the classroom door, Mr. Smith walks to his desk. He is tall, thin, bald, and wears glasses, a typical teacher's look. Still, it becomes apparent quickly that Mr. Smith is fading and fading fast.

"Take out your books, and let us start out on... um, chapter three, page seventy-two. Stacey, will you read and then go around the room, taking turns? Switch it up every five pages." Mr. Smith looks down at his papers, appearing to be busy grading papers or something. Stacey reads. Will, one of the new acquaintances, is sitting at the desk in front of me fidgeting. Will is my age, dark hair long overdue for a trim and rough on the edges. Messy with his ripped jean jacket, makeshift AC/DC patches sewn on, and a rectangle boxed item is bulging, probably cigarettes, in his front jacket pocket.

Will turns around and says, "So what are you doing this weekend, Miller? My brother got me some Chocolate Thai Stick that is phenomenal."

"Really? Chocolate Thai? Does it taste like chocolate?" I ask.

Chuckling quietly, he answers, "No, not really, but it gets me baked," he says, really hitting the 'ay' in baked for emphasis. "One bong hit, and I'm whacked out. Friday night—you want to meet up?" Will asks. This is my chance, he has weed, and I am invited to the party, yes!

"Yeah, man. I am free. Where do you want to meet?" I ask with eager anticipation.

"I don't know?" Will answers. "How about the library, at seven, I'll be inside? I have some shit to do. Just do not be late, boy. I will not wait around all night for you."

"Okay. That is cool. Library at seven." I respond. Whoa, this will amaze—finally, someone to hang with. We hear students laughing suddenly.

"Look at him!" laughs Will. The entire class laughs simultaneously. Stacey stops reading and sits up straight, holding her index finger to her lips, looking right at Will as she urges.

"Sh-don't wake him up!"

24

The entire class chuckles, we all watch Mr. Smith nap in his chair, his head tilts to the right. Amazingly, he does not even fall over. Staying perfectly in position sitting up in the chair, our teacher, Mr. Smith, slept. The rest of my school week was dull. I could not think of anything besides Friday. I could not wait to hang with my new friend and smoke some weed for the first time.

Friday night arrives, and I ride my bike up the block to the West Islip Public Library. It is just starting to get dark and chilly outside. I pull my *Jets* hoodie down over my ears. It is cold. Bundled up, I feel excited to hang out with someone new for once. Walking in the front door of the brick library inside it feels nice and warm. Will meets me right as I walk in?

"What's up, man?" he says as he slaps me on the back. "Let's get out of here." He struts back out the door.

"Oh, okay. Where are we going?"

"Shit, son…" Will says, shaking his head back and forth. "You must not know me very well. Where are we going? We're going to puff a fatty that's where we're going… duh."

"Okay, cool. I'm cool with that." I announce. I am going to smoke pot for the first time. Am I cool with that? Yes, I am! We walk outside. I pop the kickstand up on my standard ten-speed that has handlebars that twist upward. I swing my leg over the back and sit, ready.

"Let's go!" He shouts from his bike and then pulls out his Marlboro Red cigarette pack and a Zippo lighter. Whoa, Marlboro Reds, yikes, nasty. He smacks the box on his left wrist. He pulls one cigarette out, sticks it in the side of his lips, holds it steady, and snaps back his Zippo lighter, striking fire, he lights it up. With a few quick pulls on the end of the cigarette, then a long draw in, he lets out a big exhale of billowing smoke.

He peddles his bike so fast I take a few minutes to catch up. I finally get close enough, and he slows down.

"So, where are we going?" I yell and gasp for air, trying to keep up on my bike. He just stays on a mission. I still cannot keep up. He practically flies, peddling behind Good Samaritan Hospital, and then makes a right down to the beach fields near the pier. Finally, he stops up ahead. Ten seconds later, I join him. My hands and my nose feel frozen at this point.

"Dude, you busted out of there like a maniac. You left me in the dust." I pant, hands holding my knees while trying to catch my breath.

"Try to keep up, Miller. You need to work on your cardio," he says, laughing out loud. "I'm just busting your balls, man. But still…"

"Yeah, yeah," I snap back. "Just light that thing up already. I don't have all night." I toss my bike to the side and stand in front of Will, waiting. It was dark at the beach fields, and you can see a few boats out near the pier. We are the only two people anywhere.

"Okay, man, you're right, you're right. Here you go." Will hands me the joint and lighter and says, "You, my friend, may have the first and tastiest toke."

"Thank you, sir, thank you, sir. Don't mind if I do, don't mind if I do." Fumbling with Will's Zippo lighter, I strike a friendly fire, and I take my first puff. Softly, I draw in the vapor. Tasty, peppery, sweet. I hold it in and then exhale. I do not cough.

I give a few lips-smacks of approval and declare, "delicious. Tasty. Thank you." I pass the doob to Will. "So, chocolate Thai Stick, huh?" I curiously wonder.

"That's what my brother 'phat-deek' tells me anyway," Will

says.

"Fat dick?" I ask.

"No, 'phat-deek,'" he emphasizes the 'e' letter. "My brother, the biggest and phattest of deeks in this world, and I can't wait until he goes to college and gets the hell out of my house!"

"Yeah, I have an older skinny deek of a brother, and I hope he moves out for good. At least he's away at college most of the time now."

"They're all deeks," Will says. "All a bunch of deeks!" He yells. We nod our heads in agreement. We puff and pass the doobie until it burns Will's finger, and he throws it down. I feel terrific. We shake hands and part ways for the night, but I have a good feeling I will see him again. Finally, someone cool who thinks I am cool too. As I pull up in front of my house, I still feel amazing. I am nicely baked and feel optimistic about my new friend, Will. This is a first. I put my bike away in the garage, go inside my house, and I am hit with my mother's voice that snaps me back to reality. Oh, my god. I hope I do not stink or look high. Shit, shit… my mind is racing with fear of being busted. What will they do…?

"Hey, Kevin, what did you do tonight?" my mom asks from across the room.

I duck my face down a bit and answer, "Nothing much; I went up to the library and met my friend, Will, there. I know him from school," I say nervously. My mom walks by me. She reaches out and grabs my face.

She looks concerned and asks, "What's wrong with your eye? Did you get something in it? What happened?"

I step back out of her grip and answer, "Yeah, a bug flew in it when I was riding my bike. I was going fast when it hit me." Oh my god, she knows. She knows…

"Wow, that stinks," she says, "Maybe you should go take a shower and rinse out that eye while you're at it, honey."

"Yeah, that's a good idea," I confirm as I sprint upstairs and go into the bathroom. I close the door and pause while my heart stops pounding and go right to the mirror to look at myself. I turn my face to the right to see my left eye up close, and I can see right away my left eye looks red and lazy.

"Oh, my god. That is not good," I whisper under my breath. Not good at all. Overall, great time with Will, though... great time.

6

Shenanigans

Will and I hang out every weekend now; we are always high and ride our bikes around the town of West Islip, NY. We love cruising around while listening to AC/DC, Led Zeppelin, and Ozzy with our matching Sony Walkman portable cassette players. So many great songs, *Bon Scott* is a revelation, and *Diary of a Madman* by Ozzy is the most abused cassette tape I own. When I hear Led Zeppelin, though, I go to another level.

We have established routines in the middle of all the mayhem in my neighborhood. My parents dislike Will; they believe he is a dirtbag, loser type, and I should not hang out with someone like him. I rebel. Will and I are smoking pot and getting into trouble all the time. I call it the pot life; it draws me toward what I think I want, only to lose it altogether, eventually. It is like a shadow ever-present just on the other side of the daylight.

Will and I are so bored, and it is Halloween, so, as is tradition, we stockpile eggs and shaving cream; we set up egg-ammo hiding spots all along our bike route for reloads. We wait, sitting on our bikes for unsuspecting kids to pass by, and immediately see an opportunity for an attack.

"Get 'em!" Will yells as we spin our bikes around and start peddling hard toward the kids. The kids see us coming and try to outride us. It is no use; they ditch their bikes and try to run around the side of a house. We jump off our bikes and chase after them while spraying them down with shaving cream. They are screaming and dripping with eggs and shaving cream, and we are just laughing hysterically. Out of nowhere, a firm hand grabs the two of us by the arms and drags us into a garage; a man yells at us.

Fuming and red in the face, he scolds, "What the hell is wrong with you kids? Look at you guys. You are a mess! And look at the mess you made all over my yard. You guys are going to clean all this shit up right now!" as he points to his yard, hands shaking. He tells us what terrible kids we are and how he is going to call our parents. His grip on our arms is still tight. My heart is pounding.

"You know what, I'm going to call the police on you two idiots. Don't move from this spot," he shouts as he lets our arms free and goes toward the side of his garage. He presses the garage door button and then angrily stomps inside his house. The garage door closes. We both look at each other and immediately sprint to go out, ducking down; we just make it under as it shuts. We run to our bikes and book it. I never look back. A minute of fast-moving left and right turns, and we both finally show up together and start laughing out loud.

"What a clown that guy is!" Will says.

"I'm going to have an enormous bruise on my arm here. Holy shit," I complain, pointing to my left bicep. "That guy is strong as fuck."

"Yeah, Fuck that guy! He just made it to my list!" Will

responds with defiance. "He just made it to the top of the list!"

"The List?"

"Yeah, the list," Will says. "When some rubberneck like that guy does something like that... that's how you get on the list!" My arm hurts like hell, and I am in complete agreement with Will on this one. Fuck this guy! We get back on our bikes and cruise near the old guy's house again. Will gets an idea. It cannot be right.

"This way." he says, "down this block is the most beautiful puppy farm you will ever see."

"Puppy farm?" I wonder.

"Just follow me, boy! I will make it clear soon enough," Will says. I follow him nervously to a house with a big landscaped yard with big smooth looking river rocks in a garden. He gets off his bike and picks one up and tosses it up, and catches it again.

"Look at this, puppy!"

This is the big reveal. "Oh, shit, dude, puppies got it. You want to throw...? A little risky, no?" I question. I felt a little worried about stirring a proverbial hornet's nest in our neighborhood.

"Fuck him!" Will snaps. "Sometimes, you learn the hard way. You fuck with Kevin and me, and you make my list! Let's go!" He gets on his bike and starts riding fast back towards the man's house.

"Dude, wait up!" I shout, peddling hard on my bike to keep up.

"Let's go. I'm not waiting around for you!" He yells back.

I put on my headphones, and AC/DC, *Problem Child,* is playing. Perfect. I never completely catch up to him. He passes the house and throws an absolute dime right through the second-story bedroom window... SMASH!

He stops his bike yells out, "Motha' fucker!"

"Holy shit!" I roar as I toss my 'puppy' at a car in the man's driveway, but it just ricochets off the side—a miss. I am petrified. I crank up the gears on my ten-speed and bust it into full panic escape mode. We keep going until we get to the back of the Library. Will gets here first and spins his bike around while laughing.

"Did you see that? Oh, I totally nailed it!" He keeps laughing, "Did you hit anything? I didn't hear."

"No, I skimmed it off the car. Dude, Will, you nailed that window. Holy shit!"

We both started laughing hysterically! "Fuck you, dude!" I say as I point my middle fingers in the general direction of the man's house. Will joins in the finger-pointing, and we just keep on laughing.

I do not know where our anger is coming from, but we both have tons of it. We are two pissed off testosterone-filled kids with nothing better to do. We have no parties they invite us to or girls we can hang out with. Our social calendars are entirely empty. We are two crazed lunatics bashing windows until late at night while cranking up our Walkman's. And, after a few months of ridiculous shenanigans, I am getting more and more desperate for some female interaction and less of this nonsense with Will.

The kids at school make fun of me, sometimes they treat me like this, total geek. I am still struggling to find a social group that I can just chill with. I like to hang out with Will, but he does not have any girls around him. Things are going nowhere fast at my high school. I determine that the football players always have tons of girls around, so I try my hardest to fit in. At school at lunchtime, one star of the football team, Chris, rips into me. He finishes talking about the excellent time he had over the weekend that I am not fortunate enough to be a part of.

"So, what did you do last night, Miller? Play darts?" as everyone at the table cracks up laughing. Yep, I am the geek of the cool kids' group, and I am too much of a wimp to stand up for myself.

My high school scene is sucking so unbelievably bad, I cannot wait for spring to come so I can get back to *the Oak Beach Inn*. I am going to change things around for myself. Counting the days down on my calendar, my parents do not want me to go back there; they know there is no stopping me.

7

The Water Rat

B ack at *The Oak Beach Inn*, spring has arrived. I am flipping pizzas for all the lovely Long Islanders that need a refreshing drink and fantastic company. Sunday fun-day is live music time. The pizza parlor is easy to work, and it is central to the action. Scanning the crowd for anything exciting, I notice two of the hottest ladies in the group. There they are. They are probably both around thirty, I would guess—the pinnacle. Actual women. Not like most of the immature little girls at school that did not like me. I am hoping, praying even, that they will have a sudden need for pizza.

They are rocking golden tans, and both are wearing ripped jean shorts. I know them, Ms. Holland and Ms. G, teachers from my high school. Three or four guys circle like vultures. Lime wedges float inside the tall glass Corona beer bottles as they giggle and mingle, utterly oblivious to the attention. They make their way through the crowd, and, before too long, more guys encircle. They seem to have a lot of fun as the group of guys follow them around like helpless little puppy dogs. I chuckle as they go outside to hang out on the deck. Being the fly on the wall can have its advantages, I ponder as I continue making pizzas.

Barbara Jane whips around the corner and yells out, "Hey, Kevin, can you please go over to the main dance floor with the rest of the guys and help them clean up the brunch station."

"Yes, Ma'am!" I stiffen up and salute. She laughs and shakes her head. I am excited to do anything different besides making pizza. I skip and clear the area with my coworkers; it did not take much time working as a team. I am finishing sweeping, bend down to scoop with my dustpan when the DJ yells out.

"Chicka-boom!" The bass pumps out. Boom, boom, boom... *Send me little Forget me nots... help me to remember...* The sound is echoing and vibrating through my entire body, chills rush, and I stand up in utter amazement. The music that flows through me on this empty dance floor is a real, life-altering moment in time.

I have seen a few guys and girls before frequently start jamming and getting down to the newly cleared dancefloor beat. These guys are working, dancing, and finding girls that are just dying to spin around. These guys come in all shapes and sizes; their shirts are all open halfway, and they all wear tight pants. The hookup master is what I will call them. Out here on the dancefloor, they shake, grab girls, and twirl them around. The girls love it; they gush with smiles. I wish I could dance like that, but I need to finish working.

Will and I, with our friend Joe from school, decide that we will cruise my boat after I finish at *The Oak Beach Inn*. I go home and head straight for the attic at my house; I am on a mission. I am grabbing a bottle of Smirnoff Silver Label out of the countless cases of liquor my parents have. They will never miss it. Over the years, mom and dad have accumulated all this stuff from the big office parties. Dad and his partner Jim throw some fantastic events.

I may not take my boat out this late, but I am doing it anyway. My parents are at work, I will be back before they return, so they will never even know I left. I hurry and change into more comfortable clothes because Will and Joe will be here soon. I throw my Deaf Leopard t-shirt and jean shorts on. They told me earlier that they will grab four cans of Ginger Ale for chasers. I go out to meet them behind the house, outback by the *Water Rat*, a twenty-two-foot Mako with a two-hundred Mariner outboard engine. Cursive writing on the side panel reads *Water Rat*. We meet and run together down to the dock, where she was securely waiting.

I pull and twist the tie ropes and push away from the dock, smooth. We all get in. The engine starts with ease as I hear the familiar low gurgle sound of the blades spinning underwater, and we cruise along the canal. I stop the boat and drift for a few minutes to do shots with the guys. We are rocking out to rad jams on the boom box. Joe pops open three cans of Ginger Ale while I pull out the vodka, shot glass, and pour the first one. I hand it to Will, and he quickly slugs it down and then finishes with a swig of Ginger Ale. I promptly do the same, and Joe follows. I guess in the moment of trying to be cool and look tough, we all just keep passing it around—another, then another. Like icing on a cake, Will pulls out a small roach, and we each take a couple puffs before it burns my fingers, and I drop it in the water.

Joe grabs the bottle and declares, "Dude, it's almost gone. Might as well finish it." I am feeling it hard as we finish the bottle. I start up the boat again and drive. With a cigarette dangling out of his mouth, Will stands up so majestically with the bottle, raising it up high with his right hand. Just as the boat gets moving, he throws it into the water as we all laugh hysterically.

Will grabs the boat wheel, and I am too dizzy to decline. Everything is hazy; I can hardly tell what is going on. He pulls out alongside what I believe is a clam boat and bumps into it, as a little old man in the ship pops up and yells at us. I am not myself and not thinking. Foggy. We are belligerent, and he punches out the clam boat's window and is bleeding all over the interior. Everything blurs; I cannot pinpoint Will or Joe. I cannot focus. Will declares he is driving us back to my house; I do not understand how. Is this a dream...? We jump out somehow and leave the *Water Rat* to take our bikes and ride up the street to a party at Julie Anne's home. I black out completely...

Then, I detect a faint familiar muffled sound, a voice, a yell in the distance.

"Kevin... Kevin... Kevin!" The voice echoes. Clunk, clunk, clunk... footsteps? Then, the familiar sound of the garage door cranking like nails on a chalkboard. Wait, where am I? Before my mind can even compute, the sunlight pours in over my limp body as the door opens slowly. Screetchhh. My head and body hurt excruciatingly, and I can hardly move, even though I want to. What the...

"Kevin! What the fuck?" my dad screams. He stomps in the garage and stops in front of my limp body face down over my Schwinn bike. I reek of alcohol, pot, and failure. He grabs me and picks me up like a rag doll and yells, "Kevin, what's going on? What happened to you?"

I do my best to stand then speak with a slur, "I *is* home by eleven-thirty."

"What?" he yells.

"I *am* home by eleven-thirty. Just like I *is* supposed to."

"Oh my god," he says. "Kevin, you have got to be kidding me. Are you okay? I saw the blood in your boat." He looks me over to see if I am bleeding anywhere, but I am not. My boat?

"Come on," he says and drags me upstairs and throws me in the shower; he cranks up the cold water, which can be chilly in New York, to sober me up. I keep slurring and repeating the time I had arrived home. My brain and mouth are not lining up to say the words I need to say.

Dad scolds, "I tied the boat up, secured it, and started looking for you, Kevin!" He pauses and then continues, "I was getting ready for work. I looked out the window to the backyard as I was putting on my jacket and saw the boat floating in the canal. I ran out there, and there were batteries all over the floor, soda cans, and who knows what else. Your mother is beside herself, too. Big break for a while, buddy." He goes on scolding as the water runs over my head and face. His voice seems to muffle. My head hurts so damn bad… I would never leave the *Water Rat* floating in the canal. What have I done? Dad gets up and walks downstairs; I hear him yelling at mom as he goes downstairs to leave for work. I feel bad I made my dad so angry, and mom upset too. I messed up bad. With zero privileges or friends, the rest of the summer is going to suck royally. This is the other side of my bad choices. This is the pot life.

8

Make a Wish

Spring on Long Island is hope, beautiful bright blue skies, and *the Oak Beach Inn* shows life after a quiet winter. Shifts start up again for me, mostly doing the deli counter or the pizza stand, like usual. I can finally get away from all these dicks at my high school, and maybe if I am lucky, I meet a girl I like. I'm tired of the pot life; I'm not saying I'm never smoking weed again, just a change of pace—no more dumb choices. Mary Jane will always be my muse. Who knows, maybe she steers me away from the wrong decisions.

Friday night barbeque at *The Oak Beach Inn,* and I arrive early, ready to work. I am operating the large grill that faces customers; I hand out free wings and thighs to smiling faces all night. Dawn, one of my long-time work buddies, comes up to me and gives me the signal. A thumb and index finger pinched together up to the duck face lips. Yeah, you know the one. I immediately respond with an *absolutely give me five* hand gesture.

Dawn is cool ass shit. She is three years older than me, and she is hot, but we are not like that for whatever reason. Maybe because we both know I have zero shot with her, anyway. So, there is no tension, just puff buddies. I meet her out the east end door, which faces the parking lot and the club entrance. They always line up in the back of the entrance, and it makes for excellent people watching. I smell it right away as I walk up, and she extends the joint to me.

"Thanks. I need this. I've been scrounging roaches for the last two days waiting to get paid; see anything you're looking for out here?" I ask. We look over at the line that is already fifteen people deep and forming more by the minute. The girls with the big hair and denim top-to-bottom matching sets and guys with button-ups buttoned-down. Such a diverse variety of interesting individuals.

Dawn gives me a look and says, "Shit, no! I do not even want to think about guys right now. My boyfriend Larry has been flaking out big time lately. I am just sick of it all! How about you?"

"Eh," I mumble as I scan the parking lot and the line. "I'm just glad I'm here instead of at one of West Islip's amazing high school bashes. No, thanks!" We continue talking, and just as I take a big sweet puff, a seed pops like popcorn, flies out of the joint, and misses my head as I duck back in the nick of time as it flies overhead.

Dawn jumps back, laughing so hard and yells, "Oh, shit! Make a wish!"

We are laughing so hard my stomach hurt. I see someone out of the corner of my eye from a distance near the line. Two girls are looking in our direction, giggling and pointing.

"Nice one!" The tall, long blond hair girl shouts.

I gasp a little in shock, "damn, that's Kristen Wolff. She used to go to West Islip for years and then sent away to some boarding school for troubled girls."

"Really?" Dawn replies. She squints her eyes to get a closer look. "She doesn't look troubled to me. She is hot, Kev." Dawn looks right back at me and lifts an eyebrow, and grins.

"I know, right, super hot," I say as I wave back to Kristen. Oh, my goodness, she is gorgeous. Kristen motions me to say that she is heading in; I wave back with a smile and a thumbs up. Okay, I nod.

"Giving her the thumbs up? That is a smooth move, buddy!" Dawn says. "Alright, time to go back in before we get fired. Or at least before I get fired. Tell me if you want my help with that one later."

"Help me? How are you going to help me with her?" I ask.

"Trust me, honey," Dawn explains, "I know girls. If she sees me touching you and talking to you, she will want you. Guaranteed." Dawn winks.

"What? No way!" I innocently respond.

"Yes, way," she answers, shaking her finger at me. "Just let me know if you want my help or not... It doesn't really matter to me!" She shrugs as she walks back inside to go back to her station.

"Okay. I'll let you know, thanks!" We split up, and I head back to my post, the grill. The free barbeque is over at seven, and I go over to the pizza station for the rest of the night. I frantically search the crowd for Kristen, but I cannot locate her no matter how many times I try. I almost give up. It is around nine, I hear someone yell out to me.

"Hey, I saw what you were doing out there. Does your manager know about your bad habits?" surprises Kristen.

"Hey," I smile shyly. "I'm allowed to smoke cigarettes on break. It's a nasty habit, but I'm working on it."

"Yeah, right, cigarettes? I've never seen a cigarette explode like that before," counters Kristen. I walk over to the edge of the counter and introduce myself.

"Hi, I'm Kevin."

"I know who you are, Kevin. I'm Kristen... Kristen Wol..." before she could get the word out, I confidently interject.

"Kristen Wolff. Yes, I know you, too." As we both laugh together, I am mesmerized by her eyes and smile. She introduces the girl I had seen with her outside earlier.

"This is my sister Sheryl," She giggles and points. They look similar, but Sheryl seems shy.

"Hi, Sheryl," I respond.

Kristen declares, "My sis' lives right down the block from here, so we can walk from her place. It makes it much safer, no driving."

I am feeling so relaxed and chill with Kristen. "So, I guess your back?" I ask, "I haven't seen you around for years."

"Yeah, I'm back to graduate from West Islip High School. I was away at a boarding school for girls, but that did not work out so well. My mom works at our high school, so she got me back in for the end of the year." She explains. Suddenly, she is getting pulled away from my google eyes, and I snap back to reality.

"C'mon Kristen, we have to go. Goodbye Kevin. Nice meeting you." Sheryl says as she drags Kristen away.

Wait, no... Kristen. "Okay, see you around," I wave as she leaves, bummer.

She is so pretty. She is one of the most beautiful girls in high school. I am lit up. This day is turning out to be fantabulous.

"Kevin, you can shut down the pizza stand now. I want to get out of here before midnight. Barbara Jane is doing the late

42

shift," shouts Bill, my manager. No more daydreaming. I agree and shut down the oven and clean my station; I head to the kitchen. I see Dawn looking for me, and she makes the hand signal again; we go back to our usual spot. She lights another joint up and starts right in.

"So, did you ever run into that boarding-school girl?" Dawn shrugs.

"Yeah, I talked to her for a minute. She remembered me. I tried to talk to her some more, but her sister dragged her away," I explain.

Dawn surmises, "You'll get nowhere with her when her sister is around." We are passing the joint back and forth, puffing away.

I agree, "yeah, it looks that way. Maybe I'll just wait until school and hope I see her in the hallway."

"No. Screw that. Let's go find her!" Dawn says as she grabs my hand and starts pulling me.

"Whoa, whoa. What are you going to do?" I wonder. I stop in my tracks and look earnestly at her hand on my arm. I put the joint out and give it to Dawn.

Dawn gently encourages, "Just leave it to me, Kev. Let's see if we can find her and if we can; just do what I tell you." We walk toward the club inside. She is not at the front bar, not on either dance floor. "Okay, let's check the deck." We walk to the door that leads to the deck bar, and I can see Kristen through the glass doors talking to people at the bar with her sister by her side.

"There she is," I say, pointing towards her.

Dawn begins, "Okay, here's what we're going to do. We are going to walk to the railing out to the right, passing her. Just make sure she can see you, but do not make eye contact with her. When you see that she is looking, just let me know, and I'll take care of the rest."

"What, uh, what are you going to do?" I ask with a confused look.

"Just trust me," she responds. "Okay, let's go." She grabs my hand and starts walking. She slowly walks along ever so calmly and looks straight ahead while pulling me by the palm of my hand. Dawn and I lean against the rail and look at each other. Kristen will see us from here.

"Okay, now what am I supposed to do," I whisper loudly to Dawn with a shrug.

She leans in and whispers in my ear softly, "Just take it slow, take it slow and in two seconds, tell me some stupid joke or something."

I have a clueless look on my face and say, "Like a long joke or just act like what?"

Dawn laughs and says, "Oh my god, you're just too much, little boy, so listen, I'm just going to laugh at your joke." She laughs out loud, obnoxiously. "You're too cute!" She shouts and continues laughing out loud and puts her hand over mine and leans in and says, "Oh yeah, Kev. I got Kristen's eyes on us now. Just another second and..."

Dawn pulls back away, laughing one more time, grabs my hand and pulls me out, heading further away from Kristen. Wait, what? How is this going to work?

Dawn stops us and smiles again as she spins around and says, "Oh, that's too funny. I have her locked in on us; she does not even know what hit her. I will tell you that right now. So funny!"

"What are you talking about? That's it? You just touched my hand." I am so confused about this inconsistent behavior.

44

What is Dawn doing, and why?

"Trust me," she responds strongly. "You're in!" She waves her hand back and forth, laughing like a mad hatter.

"You're crazy!" I say, "No way." I huff at her and shrug again. She stops and stares at me.

"Alright," she replies. "Don't believe me, but when you do your little thing with her, don't forget to thank me for all the hard work I put in for you." She leans in toward me to make her point clear and grins. We both laugh so hard.

Dawn reaches and grabs a short joint from earlier out of her bra and says, "I still have this roach. We might as well take a few hits while we're out here." Dawn winks slyly.

"Light it up," I confirm. We both look back to see if the coast is clear and then light up. We hang out and puff at the end of the dock until we see Kristen go back inside. I nod my head at Dawn.

"Well, I would just like to say thanks for getting me laid tonight. I appreciate it."

Rolling her eyes, she says, "Yeah, you thank me for that, your little wish. What about thanking me for getting you stoned three different times tonight, you ungrateful bastard!" She shakes her head at me and gives me a friendly shove. I wonder how I am going to find Kristen again. I determine that my mission will require me to arrive at school early on Monday to find her.

9

A Ticket and a Kiss

I arrive early at school, and no matter how much I try, I do not find Kristen and give up. I go through the day thinking about nothing else but her and go home feeling down. I march straight to the mail in the garage, a ritual of mine, to cut off any potentially harmful mail items that slide through the letter slot into my parents' hands.

I pick up the papers, *The Pennysaver*, junk mail... what is this? Oh no. It is a past due speeding ticket with a one hundred twenty-dollar fine. How the hell am I going to pay for this without telling my parents? Oh crap, thirty days to pay, or they will suspend my license. I need to do something. I must sell something. What? Jewelry? I have one crappy gold chain, I consider. My saxophone! That thing has got to be worth five hundred dollars or more. A pawn shop, yes, an excellent idea. Time to grab it and go pawn this sucker. I jump back in my car with my sax' and head right over to the place on Sunrise Highway. I have passed it a bunch of times before. Fifteen minutes later, I arrive and go inside the shop. I confidently greet the clerk, a chubby, older bald man, while I hold my saxophone.

"Hello, I'd like to Pawn this. How much do you think? It is in perfect shape. Around four years old, I think." I proudly present the instrument to the man; It was a gift to me from dad.

"Okay, hold on," the old chubby bald guy says. "Do you want to Pawn it, or do you want to sell it because those are two different things?"

"I guess I want to sell it; I will not be using it anymore, anyway. What do you think it's worth?" I wonder.

He pulls it out and looks it over carefully. "I'll give you one hundred," he says.

"One hundred? My dad paid like nine hundred dollars for it." I respond with disappointment.

"Well, one hundred is all I'm going to buy it for if you want the cash. Take it or leave it!" The man shrugs.

"I'll take it. I don't have a choice," I gulp.

The man stands up straight and rifles through some papers and murmurs, "Okay, then. I'll need your ID for the sales record." I pull out my wallet, open it, and hand him my license.

"Here you go."

"Thank you," he says. "Wait a minute, you are seventeen years old?"

"Yes," I confidently declare.

"Be eighteen, buddy. I cannot buy it from you. Sorry." And with that, I am screwed. Plan B, I guess.

The next morning, I make it to school early again, starting to wonder why I can't seem to find Kristen. Maybe she is not going here? Perhaps it is a dream? I wait until the first bell rings and give up and start heading in, then I hear an engine revving. I listen to tires screeching in the distance.

Then I see a red convertible corvette hugging the corner of the school parking lot, and the music is pumping. It is Kristen. My heart almost jumps out of my chest, and I totally panic. I go back into my car, and I hide. Pathetic, ugh. She parks and gets out with her friend. I am peeking over my dash, and she looks like a supermodel, like Christie Brinkley. I am petrified. She walks past my car with Katie Hemingway; I duck down; luckily, she does not notice me. They are both laughing hysterically at something. What the hell are they so happy about, I wonder? Once they go inside the school, I slowly emerge from my Monte Carlo.

I cannot believe I froze like that. I peek inside the doors of the front of the school building before I commit to entering, and the coast is clear. I make it to first-period class with a few minutes to spare. My classmates are rowdy, as usual, before the class bell rings. I put my books on my desk and go into the hallway to scan the area for Kristen. It is empty in the halls, and I am leaning against the wall when I hear Kristen and her friend laughing in the distance. The laughter is coming from around the corner. It gets louder, and then here she is. Kristen walks right up to me, almost too close.

"Kevin, hey, how are you? Katie and I are having a little morning celebration for my first day back at school." She is acting weird, and I smell alcohol.

"Hey, Kristen, what's up? It was good seeing you the other day," I say.

Katie speaks up, looking me up and down, and says, "When did you guys see each other?"

"Kristen replies, "Yeah, at *the OBI*. Sheryl and I went there the other night when I got back into town. But we need to go. I need to go to class before I get in trouble. C'mon, Katie, let's go."

"Bye, Kevin, bye…" they say in unison and continue walking. The boarding school is making some more sense now. Drinking in the morning before your first day back at school, I wonder? That is sketchy. She sure is pretty, though. Throughout the day, I daydream and think about Kristen. It is the end of my school day, and I am heading to my car; I see her walking out the back-school doors near the parking lot. I must make a move before it is too late. I jog out to my car, hoping to catch her attention again. I see her walking toward me.

"Hey, Kristen." I smile and shyly wave.

"Hey!" she says as she walks over, and we awkwardly begin a casual conversation.

"So how do you like high school? Did you ever go to this high school before? Or did you go away in middle school?" Did I ask too many questions? Shit, I just want to know everything about her.

"I was away since ninth grade, so I've never been to high school. It is okay, I guess. My mom is a teacher in this school, so I try to avoid her area. So is *the OBI* your dad's place or your family's?"

"It's my Uncle's place, so, ya, my family's place," I respond nervously.

Flirting, she says, "that's cool that you get to work there; your family is cool."

"Yeah, *the OBI* is cool, but my parents are not… they are super strict. I have a speeding ticket, and if I cannot pay it, I'll lose my license, but I'm too afraid to tell them." I assert.

"Can't you just sell something?" She replies, "You have any jewelry? I've pawned some stuff my dad gave me when I needed

49

cash." I am in disbelief. Is this happening?

"I have a nice saxophone right in my car. I tried to sell it, but I'm only seventeen, so they wouldn't buy it from me."

"Oh, you need to be eighteen, that is right, I'm eighteen..." Kristen winks.

"You are? Would you mind selling my sax' for me?" I ask with a big smile. "I'll give you a cut of the action."

"Yeah, I'll take you. You want to go now?" Kristen says. "Grab your sax'. I'll drive."

"Great. Thanks!" This is great. Problem solved; I determine. I jog through the parking lot toward my car, unlock it, grab the saxophone, and run back after her. Around the corner flies the convertible red corvette, top-down, growling loudly. She stops beside me, throws her hair back, and smiles.

"Get in," she says casually. This is amazing. I open the door and slide in the leather seat.

"The place is on Sunrise in Bayshore. Just go up two-thirty-one north." I say as I buckle my seatbelt and toss the sax' in the back seat.

Kristen shakes her head in disapproval. "No, that guy's a dick; I do not go to him. My guy Vinny is a little further out in Brentwood, but he's much cooler," Kristen advises. How does she know that?

"Vinny?... Okay," I respond with a puzzled look and a grin. Kristen floors it, and we are off. She is driving super-fast. Why not, I judge, it must be a gracious gift? A beast car like this one? I roll my eyes and giggle but continue to glance at her. The wind blows hard with the top down, her hair whips around.

She smiles, looks at me for a second, and says, "My sister and I had fun the other night when we saw you. That place is enormous."

"It is a great place," I respond. "I guess you have a fake ID?"

"Yeah, my sister's friend gave me hers. I am twenty-four! Janice Williams. Nice to meet you," she says with a cute smile and a wink.

"Janice," I say as I nod my head up and down. "Nice to meet you. Did you meet anyone interesting while you were at *the OBI*... Janice?"

"No, not really... there was this one guy that I met that isn't that bad," she says. "Kind of cute, I guess."

"Oh, yeah?" I say with a hint of disappointment. "Did you get his number?"

"Well, I was talking to him, but my sister kind of yanked me away before I had a chance to." She reaches over and pushes my knee and laughs. How could I forget my chance encounter being interrupted by Sheryl, Kristen's sister? I am picking up what she is putting down.

"That's a shame. Maybe if you went back to *the OBI*, he might be there." I give her a look that says I am serious, but she knows I know her joke.

With a flirty look, she says, "That's a good idea... maybe I will do that." We both laugh together as we whip into the parking lot and then head inside the pawnshop. She pushes the door and jingling loudly; the overhead brass bell alerts the clerk to our presence.

A man with black hair and a tight fit shirt steps around the corner and, with a gruff, says, "Hey Kristen, back so soon? I'm going to have to go to the bank to get more cash!" he says with a belly laugh.

She smiles and shrugs. "Nothing big today, Vinny. I have my old saxophone here that I am looking to get rid of. You want to look?" Kristen says.

"Yeah, sure. Let me see. Who's your friend?" Vinny asks as he looks over the sax'. I wander aimlessly around the waiting area.

"Oh, that's just a guy I met at the OBI the other day. Don't mind him," she says with a chuckle. Vinny continues to look over the sax'.

"It's in good shape. Nice. I can do one-fifty." He stands up straight and looks at Kristen.

"One-fifty? What do you think, OBI guy?" Kristen asks me over her shoulder.

"One-fifty sounds good," I tell her.

"Okay," Kristen declares. "Let's do it."

Vinny huffs and grabs the cash and hands it to her. Counting the twenty-dollar bills. Twenty, forty, sixty, eighty, one, one-twenty, forty, and ten is fifty. One fifty! I already have your ID on file, so you're ready," Vinny affirms.

She folds the money wad and stuffs it in her jean pocket and says, "Thanks, Vinny. You are the best. I'm sure I'll be seeing you again soon." She waves and smiles as we push the door open and the bells overhead tinkles again as we walk back to her corvette.

"I believe it!" Vinny shouts back as the door closes. We just look at each other and smile. Sweet. I open my door and say under my breath, "Thank you, Dawn."

"What?"

"Thank you, Kristen!" I shout.

"You're welcome." We rip out of the parking lot, and we are back on the highway. I think she is such an exciting and unusual person. We pull into a parking spot and park the car in front of a gas station. She pulls out the wad of cash and hands it to me.

"I'll take my cut now." Putting her hand out toward me with a smile.

"Oh, okay. How much do you want?"

She smiles and says, "What does a six-pack cost? Give me ten. I have to get some gum too, don't want mom smelling my breath." I count out my cash and give her a twenty. "Thanks. Stay here," she says, and she goes inside. I am a little nervous; she is so pretty; I watch her in the store. Do not blow this. Do not blow this. Just breathe. Breathe.

She comes back out with a six-pack of Michelob and a pack of Fruit Stripe gum. I love that gum, too. She gets in casually and drives us to the end of Eaton Lane, where you can park and look out at the Great South Bay. She puts in Depeche Mode *Just can't get enough* plays. We pop open a beer and stare out at the water. I pull out a perfectly rolled joint.

"Do you?"

"Yes, I do," she says. We laugh together, and I light up the doob. We take a few light hits, and I put it out. Now I am stoned. Things get a little quiet. I am getting nervous, and the weed is making it worse. The conversation feels forced. I am choking on my words.

Kristen breaks the silence. "We better get back. I have to drop you off at your car and then head home." We cruise to the school, and she pulls up next to my car. I look at her, and I feel genuinely grateful for her help and the great time.

I shrug and say, "Thanks for helping me out. You saved me. So, I guess I'll see you at school tomorrow?" I pull open the door handle of the car, I fumble for my keys.

"Hey, wait," she says. She gets out of her car and walks around the back and over to me. I turn around, and she grabs me with both her hands around my back and pulls me towards her.

"Not even a kiss?" she asks.

I put both my hands around her waist, pull her close to me, and our lips connect. Like an explosion of fireworks, I feel amazing. It is my first actual kiss. I love this. Is this love, actually?...

10

Sand Dunes

Kristen is my world. In an instant, I go from the kid with no chance to the cocky dick dating the unknown hot girl who drives a brand-new red convertible corvette. Now that I have Kristen, I do not need anyone else. I no longer struggle to go to all these parties, just praying for a chance for a girl to notice me. Now I can hang out with Kristen and drop in on the parties to show everyone else up. Many football players are in disbelief, and I can see their dislike for me grow.

It is a few weeks before graduation, and our friend Bill's parents are out of town, so, as tradition, he is having a party. Bill's parents' house is beautiful and big, right on the water. He has a crazy Olympic style pool with a diving board you can adjust with super spring. Sweet setup.

Kristen and I drive her car to the party, and as we drive past looking for a spot, we pass football dudes Jerry and Mike. I have sunglasses on and pretend I do not see them, but they most definitely see us. They look at each other with disgust and keep on walking. We park down the street and walk around the left side of Bill's house to the back. I grab two cups from the entrance, and we head to the Keg line. Will walks right over to us.

"What's up, guys? Hey Kristen, how are you doing tonight?" To see Will at a high school party is rare. He is here at the party because it is Bill's house and we are all mutual friends.

"What's up, Will!" I say.

"Sup Tite, should I call you Ms. Tite, Kristen?" This is his nickname for me; I would always drive and always ask for gas money. Tight with money, I suppose.

Kristen asks, "Tight? What is that?"

Will jumps in to answer, saying, "That's just our pet name for our good buddy Kevin here." Will puts his arm around me.

She laughs and says," Uh, ok, you guys go with that. I'm going to get a beer." We all go together and surround the keg; I grab the handle and start pumping.

We are near the in-ground Olympic pool's deep end, and I am staring at the giant diving board. Out of nowhere, I am grabbed from behind. I struggle and drop my cup. I see Jerry in his football jersey, fumbling with my legs and picking me up. Mike, the toughest dude in school, is grabbing my arms, and they get me off the ground. They carry me towards the pool for an embarrassing dip when I hear Mike screech in my ear, and then he drops me.

I can see the look of terror on Jerry's face, and then he drops my legs. I run out of there like a scared little mouse, and I can hear Mike scream.

"Ouch, what the hell, bitch? You scratched the shit out of me! Jesus!"

Kristen yells, "Just leave him alone!"

Jerry yells back, "We're just messing around with him. You

don't have to make the guy bleed, damn."

Louder, Kristen screams, "He doesn't want to mess around with you, freaking dicks! How stupid are you guys?" She is in their face. I make my way to her car and wait. A minute passes, and Kristen arrives.

"Here you are. You ok, baby?"

I gulp, "Yeah. I guess." I give her a hug and look at her with a newfound appreciation, "Thank you so much for that. I can't believe you did that. What did you do?" She holds up her hands, flexing her long fingers as she shows me her long fingernails.

"I gave them the claws." She laughs, and I am laughing too.

"Damn, girl! I did not understand! You are super impressive; I have to say." She walks around to the driver's side and opens the door.

"So, I guess you don't want to go back in there?" She questions.

"Uh, no," I state. Kristen gets in the driver's seat and hits the convertible button, and the roof folds back and away as I stand there.

"Let's go," she says.

"Where?"

"I know a place," she answers. "Just get in."

"Yes, Ms. Tite," I say jokingly. She shakes her head in pity as she rolls her eyes at me. We drive down Montauk Highway and then head south on Robert Moses Causeway and over the first long bridge. "So, where are we going?" I ask her again.

"You'll see," she responds. *She Drives me Crazy* is playing on the radio. Kristen exits the car before the drawbridge and then goes under it; we pull into this dark spot where two cars can fit that overlook the drawbridge. She turns off the engine, and we get out. It is a beautiful starry night, and she grabs my hand

and walks me towards the bridge. As we walk underneath the bridge, we can hear the cars whizzing overhead. Kristen smiles and looks at me.

"I love that sound. The cars going over the metal grates sound like a buzz."

I respond, "Yeah, it's funky, very cool." She turns around and grabs me and starts kissing me, I kiss back, and I am just flat out stunned with this girl. That I am here with her and she likes me.

"You're amazing, Kristen. How did I get so lucky?" I profess.

She laughs and says, "Yeah, right, you're just saying that cause you want to get laid."

I cut her off, imploring, "No, I'm serious, freaking sexy as hell, and second you pull up in that car of yours and then save me from getting thrown into the pool by those douchebags! I'm not sure how you can get any better."

"How about if I get you stoned? Would that make you like me more?" As she pulls out a joint and beams with a beautiful smile.

"Oh, my goodness!" I yell, "Are you even real, or are you just an angel sent to earth to save me?" She walks back to the car and lights the joint. She opens the car door, and we both get in. We pass it back and forth while we stare at the drawbridge and listen to music that seems to match the sound of the cars rolling and buzzing overhead.

Kristen looks at me and announces, "Let's go!"

"Now, where?" I ask as she is revving the engine.

"Cap tree boat basin," she answers.

"What's there?" I question.

"Sand dunes," she answers as she drives to pull out and gets back on the highway.

"Oh. Okay," I agree. Where is Kristen going? We continue for what seems like three minutes. She drives to the far back corner of the lot and parks.

She gets out and says, "Let's go." She walks behind the car, opens the trunk, pulls out a big red and black blanket, and slams the box closed. I know that she is around six months older than me, but I think she is way more experienced. Like way, way more.

She throws me the blanket and says, "Come with me, baby." She grabs my hand and leads us up one dune and then back down over the top towards the bottom of another dune we run, and she attests, "Right here is good." So, I lay out the blanket, and we take a seat together. I place my hand on the sheet and give her a smile, motioning her to sit next to me, closer. She leans over and pushes me back, and straddles me before I even realize we are kissing; she just grabs a hold. I am shaking like a leaf. I am so nervous.

I pull off my shorts as fast as she is going, and within seconds she is guiding it in. She has it going on in every way, and just like that, I am not a virgin anymore. Ear to ear, I smile; I am instantaneously in love.

11

Prom

Prom is only days away, and I have someone to spend it with, Kristen. I had already asked a girl named Lauren a few weeks before I met Kristen, and Adam had asked Kristen. We plan on meeting up when we get to the event and ditching our dates.

Will isn't interested in the prom at all, and Bill does whatever Will does, so they are not attending. I am dressed in a black and white suit that my mom and I picked out together, and my dad gave me his limo service to use for the night. We will just have to pay the driver, Paul, for his time driving. I am dressed and ready; I snap a few photos with my parents and walk out of my house. The black stretch limo is waiting for me on the street in front. Paul, the driver, greets me, opens the back door; I get in and sit comfortably in the back seat. I give Paul street directions to pick up my prom date, Lauren, and all the guys and gals from Mike's mansion on the water. We stop at each address and one by one pack in the limo. On our way to the party, we sing and dance in unison, jamming out to Bon Jovi and Poison on the radio. I have so much fun with everyone now. Still, I expect to meet up with Kristen, so I am preoccupied with my thoughts a bit.

We finally arrive, and one by one, like a red-carpet event, step out and walk together to the front doors arm in arm with our date. We dress to the nines. The dancefloor is bumping with well dressed, almost adult children dancing *to Mony, Mony* by Billy Idol. After each chorus, the kids all shout out in unison.

"Get laid, get fucked… *Mony, Mony*… Get laid, get fucked!" All the teachers just roll their eyes. It is high energy in the room all night. I join in a group dance with our lively friends, and Kristen scoots in, singing and dancing. What a time for young people, the prom, just before adulthood, just before college or life ahead, a time of innocence. Kristen and I leave early and go back to Will's house for the rest of the night. We really did not feel like staying all night, and we just chill and relax for the rest of the weekend with friends and family. Overall, a fantastic time with everyone. People overate these events, we decide, and I just enjoy hanging with Kristen and close friends, anyway.

On Monday, after arriving at school, I see pictures posted all over a wall near the front office. I stop to look out of curiosity. I scan the wall and see nothing and start walking away. It catches my eye—a photo of Kristen and I embracing while dancing and smiling at the prom. We look great together, happy. I think this is the first time I have ever appeared in anything school-related. I smile and find my joy, my happy place; I feel like I am fitting in now, finally, just as it is all ending.

I casually grab the local *Newsday* newspaper as I leave school. I make my way through the parking lot of cars out towards my car and glance at the front page; the headline reads $48 Million a month Coke ring bust with a picture of my buddy

Mike's father. Oh, my goodness! His dad looks like they have roughed him up bad and are sitting in the back of a police car. My heart drops, and I feel terrible. I am standing in shock as I look up over the paper; I spot Mike Sr. pull right up in front of the school; he parks, gets out, and walks in to get Mike Jr. They come out and silently get in the car and drive away. I walk to my car, thinking deeply about how I will probably never see my friend again. I cannot imagine how his father made such bad choices with drugs and money, which permanently affect his life and his kid's life; who does that, I wonder?

After graduation from high school, nothing changes in my life. Kristen, Will, and Bill fog out my Monte Carlo almost every day smoking weed, and we reminisce about the good old days of high school. We all love to share stories of years gone by, we love to listen to music and enjoy each other's company. Today is like so many others hanging out with my people, friends, and kin like the kids in the movie *The Breakfast Club*, the pot life version. Our motley crew is sitting together at Will's Mom's house, high as a kite again.

"Looks like Will and I are heading up to the Catskills for our college studies. Did you tell him, Will?" says Bill. He looks at Will with a shrug. I am clueless about what they are talking about.

"Tell me what?" I ask. "I haven't heard about anything in the Catskills. What is going on?"

Will stands and shakes his head to confirm, "Yep, it looks like we're going to Sullivan," Will declares with a chuckle.

"That's right, SCCC." Bill says, "Sullivan County Community College."

"SCCC?" I ask dismissively; I recall my brother mentioning something like this to me years ago.

"Yep, SCCC, not like you're getting into an Ivy League school yourself there, Tite," proclaims Will. It all makes sense; I can move away from home. This is my opportunity.

"That doesn't sound half bad; where is this place?" My curiosity ignites now, and I remember how exceptional it was for my brother to go off to college. He found his way—time for me to pave my way too.

Will answers, "It's around two hours north, not bad at all; you and Kristen can bounce back and forth to visit each other."

"I'm in. What do you think, Kristen?" I ask curiously. I am wondering how she feels about all of this. My desire is the entire crew with me for this endeavor, and I especially want her with me.

"Sounds good to me," Kristen says with a smile. "I will come and visit you anytime you want me to." Sweet, she is in too.

"So, it's settled then," Will proclaims. "The three of us are heading to the Catskills for some serious learning!" Will cheers with Bill, and we are all high-fiving each other. I commit mentally to our next big thing, college life.

"Yeah, that's what it'll be." Kristen laughs. "Serious learning!" We laugh without a thought in the world besides friendship, fun, and the next big adventure.

The summer after is, without a doubt, the best summer of my life. It is a carefree love fest that I love every minute of. Kristen and I both have boats and live on the water. We live a fairy tale life of fun, sex, and sun. I have officially signed up for college with Will and Bill, but Kristen stays home. So, we count down the final few days before I must leave. When the time comes for me to go, Kristen and I hug for what seems like hours. I drink in every drop of feeling love, togetherness, tranquility, and peace at this moment. I will miss this.

12

Consulting Business

Six years have passed since my High School prom and graduation party. We are sitting in the same restaurant. Except now, we are celebrating my College graduation party. This does not even feel real. It feels like a dream. It all feels like yesterday as if we were just here. We are eating a steak dinner, and my parents are so proud of me, as am I, smiling and laughing together. They are praising my achievements, and I am deep in thought.

College life went so fast. What a fantastic time with friends, girlfriends, and a sprinkle of education, too. Now that I finished, what the hell am I doing with my life? How am I going to handle all of this, I wonder? In my mind, I am going from the king of the college town to a broke, friendless loser living with my parents.

I ask my parents to rent out one of their houses on the water in the next town. The place is an amazing little two-story house eight feet off the canal, so it looks like you are on a boat from inside the house. It has an oversized detached garage and room to dock a vessel up to forty feet long. They agree to let me rent it.

My father talks to me about employment through one of his office space tenants to steam-clean carpets. It is hard work, but it can get me started with making some cash. My parents lecture about bills, life, but I am adding all of this up in my head and planning my next steps.

It's months after graduation now on a sunny Saturday afternoon. I will hang out at my old fraternity brother, Christian. He lives with his housemate Jamie in a huge compound on the water. His place is close to mine, I drive over to their home, and as I approach, I hear music thumping, and the site is jumping with activity; there are people everywhere. Everyone is playing sports or riding around on jet skis out in the back or sitting around the ping-pong tables and smoking weed. I feel right at home. I knock and let myself in and walk into the house; the smell of cannabis smacks me in the face, boom! Sweet. Spicy and kind. I find Christian watching TV in the back room. He stands up and smiles. Christian not only was my fraternity brother, but he is also a black belt in martial arts. I walk up and smile.

We shake hands firmly, and I say, "What's up, brother?"

"Brother, how's it going?" Christian asks.

"Good, good, I'm trying to adjust to life after college, but I'm having some difficulty with that."

He laughs and says, "You'll figure it out; it takes some time. Are you following your dad into real estate?"

"I don't know, the thought of working weekends for the rest of my life doesn't sound great, but…"

Christian interrupts, "Yeah, but you have a solid foundation already built. That's big!"

I reply, "It helps… I am hoping I can speak with your friend

Jamie about what he's doing, his consulting business."

"Yeah, no problem. Let's go find Jamie, and you guys can talk." Christian says. Christian motions for me to follow, and we make way through the house out near the dock over the canal. There are people just hanging out and socializing everywhere. He walks up to a floating boat, and we can see some guy's ass crack moving around inside. It looks like he is working on this boat.

Christian yells, "Jamie, put that crack away and talk to my friend Kevin, the guy I mentioned to you before. Jamie pops his head up and laughs.

"Alright, alright, hold on a second. Let me finish this up." He sticks his head back down under the engine cover and yells, "OK, try it now, Billy." Billy turns the ignition, and the engine turns over, and Billy presses down on the throttle, and the engine revs. Jamie lets out a big laugh. "Nice!" Jamie yells and gives Billy a hi-five. Jamie reaches out the boat with his hands, grabs the edge of the wooden dock, jumps up out of the boat, and walks up to me.

"So, who's this?" Jamie asks.

Christian interjects, "This is Kevin, my friend; I was telling you about him before."

Jamie reaches out his greasy black hand and gives me his kung fu grip handshake, and says, "Miller?"

I smile and shake his hand back and confirm, "Yeah, Kevin."

"So, your family owns *The Oak Beach Inn*, Christian says?" inquires Jamie with a sideways look at me.

"My Uncle, Bob," I answer and shake my head.

"So, you are working there now?" He asks.

"No, not anymore. It burned me out on the place and my Uncle too. I'm looking for new opportunities now, better

66

opportunities. I hear you have a consulting business that's doing pretty well, and I wonder if I could get in on that?"

He chuckles, "Whoa... easy, easy, let's not get ahead of ourselves. These things take time. Relationships must develop, a layer of trust built..." He hesitates and turns to look at Christian and asks directly, "Do you trust this guy, Christian?" Christian shakes his head and gives a thumbs up.

"He's a brother, one of us."

"OK, well, if at some point we can get to know each other a little better and get more comfortable. I have room for one more padawan." He pauses for a moment, and just as soon as he makes it seem like the conversation is over, he asks for more detail about me.

"So, do you have a suitable location to get the operation going? You need some space. Two rooms. One for growing small clones and the grow cycle and one large room for flowering."

"Clones?" I ask. "What are clones?"

"That's how you make your plants," Jamie says. "You cut the small under branches off, dip them in some cloning solution and put a cover on them to keep the moisture in, and then in a week, they grow roots of their own. You plant those and start the growing cycle. They will need eighteen hours of light per day. Once those plants get to a certain height, you move them into the flowering room at twelve hours of light per day and give them room to grow up and then out. Then sixty to seventy days later, they are ready for harvest."

"I have a setup for that." I say, "I have a good-sized growing and clone room and an enormous garage for flowering. So, it sounds like it can work. How do we do profit sharing? How does all that work?" I cannot believe what is happening. He is telling me all I need to know.

"It's a fifty-fifty operation," Jamie says. "I supply all the plants and equipment, lights, light movers, hydroponic solution, pumps, and you supply the location and the electricity. I'll come by occasionally to check on things and teach you the ropes. Especially in the beginning, when you don't know what you're doing, I'll be around a lot." Jamie packs his tools and supplies to walk back up the dock and to the house.

I quickly respond, "that sounds great, I have space and the time, and I could sure use the cash. I'm in. When can you come over to look?"

"I think I'm free next Monday afternoon," He says. "You or Christian can give me your address and phone number. Normally I like to vet any potential partners, but if Christian says you are good, you're good."

"Outstanding. Thanks, man." I say. Jamie whistles sharply. A big, muscular, pretty Pit-bull dog comes trotting up, turns around, and sits as it leans against my leg. She has this shiny, reddish-brown, short-haired coat that is beautiful.

Jamie laughs and says, "Oh, looks like she likes you." He talks to the dog like it is a baby, "Are you saying hi Ruby? Are you saying hi to your new friend? Yes, you are." Jamie says to the dog. I am scared, shit-less. I have never met a Pit-bull breed of dogs before, but I sure as hell hear the stories about them. This dog feels like one hundred pounds of pure muscle, and she is just leaning on my leg with her lower back. I timidly start petting her and ask, "Ruby is her name? She's so pretty." I think she is, at least. Ruby, I pet her again, and she turns and looks at me with a goofy smile.

13

The Onion

I have been thinking back to college a lot lately since seeing Christian again. Especially remembering being part of the Tau Kappa Epsilon or TKE men's fraternity. The funny thing about fraternity hazing and pledging is how the fraternity brothers progressed with their hazing ever so gradually. They don't just smash you over the head with it. Oh no, it's more of a slow timed introduction to pain and humiliation one tick at a time. Every day the fraternity brothers would get a little more intense, making you do just a few more things, just a few more push-ups as punishment.

Back in college, Christian was the fraternity president that later became part of the tribe of best friends. Like my family, dysfunctional family. I deem it is curious how things happen in life, with me meeting Jamie the other day.

I remember one glorious heyday back then in college; we were new fraternity pledges lining up outside the fraternity house. It was the third week of pledging, and we still did not have a full understanding of what hazing was. We were about to find out.

"Welcome, gentlemen, welcome. So glad you have graced us with your presence. It brings me such great joy to see you all here today." Christian spoke so articulately—every word with such precision and clarity. "I'd like to congratulate our pledge class on entering your third week of pledging. Excellent work on that. I'd also like to congratulate all our brothers with us here tonight for that third-week milestone. So, without further ado, I would like to say to all you scum here today, I'm going to need you to…"

He pauses momentarily, takes a huge breath, and yells, "Get your worthless asses to PNC grocery store and pick out the largest onion you can find!" What? His voice and words' pace got louder and faster, like a bomb getting ready to explode or a clock ticking slowly before the alarm blares out. His face turns red like a tomato against his blonde hair, and he screams even more emphatically.

"Let's go, losers, don't think I haven't already checked the onion selection to identify what the biggest onion looks like… alright, smart guys? Let's go! Now! Now!" He points toward the door, and we scramble frantically, grabbing for our backpacks, we sprint out.

I recall I didn't know my other pledge brothers that well, yet. I knew some of their first names, but they had given us all pledge names through the fraternity. We were like chickens with their heads chopped off; like fools, we run to the PNC grocery store. We looked like crazed lunatics running around toward the produce section.

"Oh my god, look at the size of this one!" Says Gonzo, as he held up a medium-sized yellow onion.

"What the hell?" Monchhichi says as he grabs a much smaller red onion. "Don't pick that one dude, that thing is way too big;

let's take this one."

"I don't think we should take the small one," I declare fearfully. "Did you hear what Christian said about already coming here and finding the biggest one?" I shrug my shoulders; that is what I believe he said.

"We don't have time for this shit, man," Queef says as he grabs the massive yellow one out of Gonzo's hands. "Let's get the hell out of here!" He holds the onion high like a prize as he runs to the counter; through the aisles, he quickly makes his way to checkout. He hands the woman the onion and money, and we catch up to him to pile in line behind.

"This is fucking weird," whines Nyquil. "Why are we even doing this?" We were panting to catch our breath from jogging. Shit, would we make it back in time? Gonzo grabs his change and receipt, and we run out together like a herd of wild animals. We haphazardly make our way to the front of the fraternity house, where the brothers were waiting for our return. We shove and run inside the house.

"You are fucking idiots!" Loops shouts. "Seventeen minutes douche-bags, seventeen minutes. Who has the onion?"

Paul steps up and says, "I have it, sir," and looks at Loops with a proud half-smile.

"Don't eyeball me, Queef! What are you, stupid? Could you give me that onion? Now back down in work position!" Work position is when you lie on your back and raise your feet off the ground and hold that position. Lucky for me, I was skinny and in OK shape. Still, some of my other pledge brothers are not so fortunate and will struggle vigorously. Their legs shake and move around radically, making them specific targets for all the brothers standing over them.

"Holy shit, Monchhichi! Are you fucking kidding me? Three

seconds in, and you're already falling out of position? Pathetic! So, dicks, you are two minutes late, so let's start with two minutes of work position."

All of us get down but are struggling after twenty seconds. Loops goes on speaking slowly.

"So… welcome to week three; you worthless pieces of scum. I hope you realize that the beginning of pledging has now concluded, and you are in a new stage. A much more exciting stage that allows us brothers to spread our wings and explore our more creative sides. Legs up, Monchhichi! Your way too soft for this, Monchhichi, wouldn't it be easier to give up, quit?"

"No, sir!" Monchhichi shouted back as he struggled forcibly to keep his feet off the ground.

"Look at you, losers!" Loops resumes after a few seconds of pause. "You guys are all a bunch of freakin' out of shape, dumb asses, weak. Get up now!" He shouted, "Head to head, go, go!" He paces back and forth, observing us.

We all jump to our feet and get back into line tightly packed, lined up with our forehead pressing against the back of the other guy's neck.

"Side to side!" He roars and sways. "Take this Rainman," and he hands the sizeable half-chewed onion to the tallest pledge at the unfortunate end of the line. "Take a bite and pass it along." Rainman takes a huge bite and passes it.

Loops continues, "Big bites, ladies, big bites. Eat our delicious TKE vegetable. Do not stop until you finish." He sways back and forth, almost a cult-like rhythm.

I can see the large onion handed to each pledge standing in the line. One by one, the coughing and sniffing would follow down the path. Each committed bite would cause these grown guys to lean forward and start hacking and wheezing. The onion arrives at my position, and I try to sneak a small bite—a big mistake.

"Are you kidding me, Clap?" Clap is my pledge name. It turns out someone knew an old girlfriend of mine from the year I had gotten the Clap, also known as Gonorrhea. Who knows how it all happened? But someone found out about my alarming situation, and Clap became my pledge name. Loops shouts out as I try to pass it along.

He gets in my face and yells, "No, Clap. Take another bite. A real one." I draw in a deep breath and make a large bite this time—another mistake. I spat and gagging on it. Loops goes berserk.

"Are you kidding me, Clap? You must kid me. There's no way you're wasting our glorious vegetables, fifty push-ups now."

I drop to the floor, coughing and gagging, and start pushing my body's weight off the ground.

"One sir, two, three…" I was spitting out the onion and gasping for air, barely keeping down the vomit.

Loops stands back up, and all the other brothers start in on us.

"Let's go!" They roar.

"Eat, eat, eat, eat!" They are all joining in.

"You guys suck!"

"You're never getting in, never!" The brothers are laughing loudly and slapping each other on the back in approval.

"Oh, it's just too easy, guys, too easy!" The laughter practically shakes the floor.

"OK, OK, that's it for tonight, brothers. That's it! Fun's over for tonight. Let's break it up." With that, it was over. It was slightly traumatizing, and that was not all the crazy events that happened, but I am glad I kept in touch with Christian after all this time. I never realized what an impact the camaraderie or feeling of familiarity was for me. I reflect and decide, you never know, that anything can lead to everything in life, sometimes.

14

High Times Magazine

C hristian and Jamie go half on the price of a forty-foot Cruiser's Inc. boat, a world-class premier boat brand. The ship is just amazing. We cruise the Bay together all the time now and hang out at some fantastic restaurants and bars. Yesterday I drove the boat and cruised over to Matthews Seafood House on Ocean Beach, Fire Island, secreted away behind a fish market. Some people never even know about this spot, and there were such magnificent breathtaking views of the Great South Bay. I carefully drove the huge boat up to the wooden dock, the water was a little rough, and the tide pushed us around, lapping the boat's sides. Patron onlookers watched as some guys appeared on the pier out of nowhere, leaping through the air with ropes in hand. They quickly got our boat under control. They lock it down to the dock space, cords tied. Jamie tips the well-deserving daredevil dockhands. We step out on the dock to have some fantastic cuisine and even more lovely views from the outdoor dining area looking over the water. We are relaxing, waiting for drinks, and I am reminiscing.

I remember Jamie helped me get set up a few years ago, and it only took two weeks to be up and running in my brand-new state-of-the-art growth room. I remember like I was there again. Eighteen hours of light per day, the plants were so tall it was already time to turn the lights back to twelve hours a day to start the flowering cycle. I remember feeling amazed at how the plant's leaves reached for the UV lights. It was like you could almost observe them growing. They looked so healthy and were growing so fast I have honestly never seen anything like it. No one can deny the beauty of this plant.

As time went by, I settled into a routine. I checked the herb every morning and again at night. I educated myself on growing. I found an article that said playing music to the plants helps their growth and vitality. Another piece that said sports talk radio got even better results than music, so I switched over to WFAN sports radio. Maybe that is just me loving to listen to sports radio. Mike and the Mad Dog were at the height of their popularity, and I am proud to have had my plant-friends listening.

After seventy-five days of tending to my beauties, it was time to snip them. The buds had gotten so huge that I had to reinforce all the plants with fishing lines to keep them from falling over. Absolute sticky-icky beauties they were. I hung them upside down and waited around five days for them to dry out. The waiting was unbearable. I plucked one small bud that seemed almost dry and attempted to smoke it, but that was a flop.

Another day and they were finally ready for consumption, and oh my lord, was I excited. Never have I nurtured something so feverishly and spent so much time and effort. All of my dedication, coming together and manifesting itself into my favorite thing of all, Mary Jane, and at long last, she was waiting.

I look closely and choose the most precise, crystal-filled flower I can discover, and I use a scissor to trim it gently. The smell is so pungent and fresh; I almost slip away into a paradise. I twist up a fatty with some bamboo papers, spark it up, and puff. A few lips smack of tasting for flavor and then a big, long exhale. Ah, oh my, was that tasty—freshly grown, farm-to-lips freshness. My pride has never been more significant than in that moment. Two very enthusiastic thumbs up! I can barely contain myself.

I call Jamie right away and tell him they are ready for sale. He drives by the next day, and we weigh all of it out. My first twenty-four plants yielded just short of one-hundred and thirty ounces—the going rate for Bud A on a wholesale level is four hundred to four-hundred fifty dollars an ounce. Then, I split half with Jamie as per our agreement. After two weeks, he had already sold it all, and my cut was around twenty-four-thousand dollars. For a twenty-four-year-old that had never had over five-thousand dollars, it was like I had struck it rich. I now must figure out what I was going to buy. It didn't take long to decide on a boat. I spent eight-thousand dollars on a nineteen-foot Bayliner with a one-hundred twenty-five horsepower outboard engine. Nothing too fancy, but it had a little cabin upfront, which was perfect for sleepovers on Fire Island. I am on my way now.

Jamie has shown me the ropes with my state-of-the-art indoor grow house, and we are doing rather well. We have had some difficulties with pests and mistakes made in the growing process over time, but, overall, it has been fun, and I'm doing well financially. Jamie and I have become close friends. He is accommodating with any issues or problems; He has a vested interest. Jamie fancies himself a singing man and is always cracking jokes and randomly sings everywhere we go, belting out songs out of nowhere. He is quite the character. We had a great time joking, eating great food and drinks, and talking about the pot life before heading back home.

That year, along with my father, I had started a mortgage lending company where we were getting most leads through my father's real estate business. A reliable business idea, I concluded, and maybe even a long term solution to my lack of what I considered respectable employment. I am not getting out of the pot life or anything, but perhaps it is possible one day. Jamie does not seem to have any concrete long-term goals in my judgment.

During our meal at the seafood house, he tells Christian and me he took pictures of his vast outdoor ganja plants and tried to get them published in High Times Magazine. Jamie develops the film himself to avoid being turned in by a pharmacy photo department cashier, but I am concerned for him. I feel he may get too flashy.

I need to make enough money to put a down payment on the house of my dreams and maybe even start another business all my own, but what will I do? What should I do? I want to hang out with my friends and feel authentic. I enjoy cannabis cultivation, but this risky pot life cannot last forever, and now it feels super dangerous.

With my new mortgage career taking shape, my father tells me I need to do a significant upgrade on my wardrobe. He sends me to his suit guy on Montauk Highway in Bayshore. I get measured up and pick out four standard suits and some other random dress shirts, pants, and ties. I know I need to fit into this lifestyle and resemble it, and I am, but it is not me, not what I love. I reluctantly reach to pay the cashier after what seems like hours of the fitting. The cashier tells me dad paid for it all, much appreciated.

I am going through the new suits at my house, putting together a few outfits, trying them on when my phone rings. Who could this be? I run down my hall to pick up the telephone hanging in the kitchen with a curly cord that stretches and drags on the ground.

I pick up the phone piece and say, "Hello?"

"The cops just arrested Jamie!" I hear Christian yell in a panic at the other end of the phone line.

"What?" I almost drop the phone, and my mind races. What and how did this happen?

Christian says, "Yeah, they came to the house around two hours ago, I was not there when it happened, but he got arrested."

I yell out, "Holy shit, did they bust him for having weed?"

Christian answers fearfully, "Growing, he is in jail for growing weed."

"Growing weed? At one of his home-grow partner's houses?" Like mine, I wonder in terror.

Christian answers, "No, dude, for growing on the boat, the police confiscated our boat, that jackass, what the fuck!" The loud, stretched-out word, fuck, reverberates in the telephone's earpiece, and I pull the phone off my ear for a second in hopes he cools off.

I am shaking in fear and reply, "They took the boat? That is brutal. I'm sorry, man, that sucks."

Christian returns and says, "So, I heard a credible rumor that Jamie's girlfriend brought some rolls of film to CVS. A worker notified the local authorities about a bunch of pictures of large marijuana plants. The cops got his address and phone number right on the customer slip." Christian is so disappointed about their boat and all the crazy intensity. I feel so bad for him. Jamie is mostly a good guy and does not deserve the punishment he is looking at, maybe a year or worse. A year in prison for growing some plants on a boat? I surmise the punishment does not fit the crime, and I honestly think Jamie will never be the same, no matter what happens. I am on the lookout now and paranoid about getting busted; I will conclude this hazardous pot life promptly following several more harvests.

15

Little City on the Water

March 2000 and we are off; I get an invitation to go out to Arizona with Dennis and Christian to visit Billy, our mutual friend and fraternity brother. We are flying out west for some fun and some sun. Billy meets us at the airport with his full-size white Bronco, and we load up to head to the hangout. He brings along his latest girlfriend to show off, I suppose. I shrug and think how great it is to get out of the New York cold and funk somewhere sunny and new. The Arizona landscape differs slightly from the east coast.

I am with Karen now. We decided a while back that Karen, my girlfriend, would move into my Long Island place with me. She drove up from Tampa to see me. She landed a job with a personal injury attorney, like the job she was doing in Tampa. It all seems to work out smoothly, effortlessly, and it is an exciting time for us.

Karen was born in the mountains of Barranquitas, Puerto Rico, and moved with her family to Tampa at seven; Karen spoke no English. She has lived in Tampa her entire life since then. I went down to Tampa to visit her for the first time, right before Hurricane Georges. I met her family in Tampa when we first started dating; they were having a big gathering at her Uncle Renee's house. We pulled up out front of his house, and it was shocking how many people there were, and I was even more amazed that there was such diversity. Karen and I are together now. It was so refreshing to experience such acceptance; I'm just a white boy from Long Island. Even though we may seem different and come from other places, this family experience felt affirming. I love being around her family; I think and feel well-received, no matter what.

I met sisters Carmen and Jeanette, her Uncle, and Stepfather too. She has one older brother Dapo and two younger brothers, Jesus and Clairance, Drew's kids. Her Mom does not speak very much English, but she is also very nice. Overall, I am astonished by how friendly everyone is to me. Everyone takes the time to talk to me, and it makes me feel appreciated. Not what I am expecting, but it is a warm family and a grateful experience. I am happy with her, but she stays in New York while I travel this time, and she will pick me up at the airport when I return.

I am almost ready to land in Arizona for a much-needed break right now. We party day and night, non-stop, I eat fresh grapefruit off the backyard trees, and we chill in the sun while getting baked all day smoking beautiful ganja weed. I meet one of Billy's friends, Chris, who recently moved out here from New Jersey. The guy seems so content in his new home, away from the northeastern winters' gloom and doom. I had to ask.

" Chris, you just moved out of New Jersey?"

"Yes, dude, yes. Best decision I ever made," he says.

"It looks that way. Everyone here seems so happy. It's hard not to notice that." I acknowledge.

"Man, I was living in Jersey, busting my ass at a medium-size financial company. I worked long hours and made substantial money, but there were so many days I never even saw the sun. I would get in before it came up and would leave the same way. In the dark. One day I was at my breaking point and said, fuck this! I would not watch my life fly by and still be busting my ass in Jersey and be miserable. I called up some friends I knew out here and asked if they had a place for me; three weeks later, I am here. I'm not making anything near the cash I used to make back there, but the quality of life is off the charts. I'm staying, and I'm never going back! Except to visit, in August." He lets out a big laugh and remarks, "I'll go back in August!"

"I think I see your point." I said, "It's time for a move; I feel like I'm finishing with New York." Arriving at the airport to head back home, I could not stop thinking about moving away to a warmer place. Those guys all get to continue their extraordinary lives while I must go back to shit-Ville, New York. No way!

Karen pulls up, and I get in the car; I blurt out, "We have to move out of this boring ass place and move somewhere warm."

"Oh my god, thank god!" Karen said. "I can't take it anymore, either!" She is so excited and clapping.

"Where do you want to go, North Carolina, maybe?" I propose.

She quickly replies, "Tampa, I can move back to my family, and the weather is so nice. You'll love it there; I think my Uncle Renee has a place that we can stay. It's two bedrooms and one bath."

"Really, Tampa? I guess that makes sense." I determine every time I see a football game in Tampa; it looks like so much fun and excellent entertainment value."

"It is nice, even when it's not nice in Tampa. Trust me, it's still nicer than it is here! Yes, let's do it, let's do it!" She claps her hands over and over.

"Alright. Let's do it. Let's move to Tampa. One thing is for sure; I can't stay here anymore."

We hug for a bit before leaving, and I could already feel the excitement rushing through me. I cannot stop smiling, and I am finally going to do something better with my life. With Karen, something tells me not to let her go. She does not know the details of my pot life yet. I plan to finance this move; soon, there will be no extra money coming in from the weed growth operation for a little time before I figure things out.

I pack up my Pitbull Peachy, Ruby's runt puppy, and my cat Mush, and we are off. The thrill of leaving Long Island's cold winter and arriving in warm sunny Tampa is extraordinary. A brand-new commencement and new life in a great little city on the water, Tampa, Florida.

16

Reminiscing

During this move to Tampa, I cannot help but think back, recollecting my college years. I admit I cherish college living, but I hated college itself. I did not know what I was looking for when I was attending college. I knew that I needed to finish, at least that's what my parents and society told me. I determine to complete it, but what did I want to do? Oneonta's courses were challenging. I had a hard time balancing being a full-time frat brother and partier, plus a full-time college student. Going out six nights a week, succeeded by my self-imposed Sunday *dry out* day, no drinking for me. Smoking weed was acceptable; I figured I owed it to my liver to give it a Sunday break. Fraternity life was all that I imagined it would be, and if I remember, I also had a brand-new girlfriend.

I was on top of the world then. Until Oneonta expelled me for a low GPA and little money to pay for extra classes out of pocket. Before Oneonta would readmit me, I needed to take additional courses to boost my grade point average. My Grandma Ronnie felt terrible for me, God rest her soul, and donated two thousand dollars for two make-up classes at Hartwick. Hartwick is nearby Oneonta, so my lifestyle did not change at all. Although I could attend, I could not afford to pay the tuition solely without help. Mom and Dad refused to pay for my mistakes. The rest would be up to me.

I needed an idea; required to brainstorm, and what better way to do that, you might ask? Smoke pot. I got in my truck and went for a quick toke and some deep thinking. I can still recall sitting under the large Oak Tree near the almost entirely deserted road. I remember I reached in my front pocket in my parked truck, pulled out my joint, and lit it up. I thought about going back home for a moment until feeling determined. I wanted to be with my friends and have fun and finish my college, too. I was not quitting.

They always say you should do what you love, and when you do, it's like you're not working at all. So what do I love? I love girls, but that costs money. I love Pot. I could sell Pot if I had the money and the connections. Wait, Gonzo can get weed. I rolled down my window and exhaled the cloud of smoke outdoors. He had scored gigantic bags before, so I believed he could do it again. I ashed the joint out the crack of the open glass as the breeze carried the embers beyond.

Now, about the money. I had around two hundred dollars from Christmas gifts. Thank you, Grandparents. I have little, but I have a brand-new Discover Card with a two-thousand-dollar limit. Obviously, you can't purchase Pot with a credit card, yet at least. Inside the envelope were two Discover checks that could go towards a cash advance to me. I took that as a sign. I endorsed it to myself for two thousand dollars, brought it to the bank, and eventually bought what I needed from Gonzo.

When I spoke with Gonzo, he told me I could get a QP

(Quarter Pound) for a thousand dollars. I bought the QP and a triple beam scale that Will's brother had, and I was game for business. The fall semester could not get there fast enough.

After completing my summer classes at Hartwick, we all got back to Oneonta; I rented a two-sided monstrosity of a fraternity house with my friends. One side was for guys, the other for the gals—me, Queef, Lenny, and my roommate Jon or JB as we call him, we're on the guy's side. On the gal's side, there were three stories and five bedrooms with six girls in total. Let me repeat six girls. I had never been more thrilled. Never.

Back then, there was an unbelievable evolution and infusion of new music that I had never heard before or since. Our local SUNY Oneonta radio station would play all this new music, and the variety just kept on coming. It started with The Smashing Pumpkins' first album. Pearl Jam's first album is the following. Then I heard Nirvana for the first time, which completely blew my mind. A Tribe Called Quest, Guns, and Roses, The Chili Peppers finished the month with new albums of their own. So much creativity going on, mostly out west. I had my theory on this massive influx of imagination.

Around the beginning of the '90s, people's access to high THC cannabis was growing exponentially. Until the '80s, weed was full of seeds, sticks, and stems mashed into bags and smuggled in from Mexico. In the '90s, California grew more and more cannabis with better farming techniques and access to proper soil nutrients. All that beautiful, sticky icky, excellent weed made its way to the masses. Mostly on the West coast. These extraordinary musical artists could expand their minds with a little help from Mary Jane, and their creativity surged. We owe a salute to those first great cannabis farmers in the mountains of California for their gift to all the music lovers like me. Still, to this day, I think of those bands as some of the best of my lifetime.

We ended up having my first fraternity meeting of the year at our enormous house on the guy's side in the basement. We discussed upcoming parties. I stood up during the meeting with an announcement.

I grabbed everyone's attention saying, "Greetings, brothers, greetings. I just wanted to let everyone know that I now have some of the finest weed on the planet, so if anyone needs anything, you know where to find me. The phone number is 433-DUDE." The fraternity guys roared with laughter at my comical phone number and high-five each other. We got a solid laugh out of that one.

I then announced loudly, "I've rolled up a few joints for you all to sample, so here you go; I'm psyched to be back. Enjoy the joints, my friends!" I handed them out and lit one up. The joints were getting passed around one by one. Everyone is receptive to the free joints, as you would expect. Paul, one of the new brothers, grabbed the joint and looked around with a big smile on his face.

He waved to everyone, saying, "Yo, later guys. It was good seeing everyone. Hope to see you again soon. Go, TKE!" Another pleasant laugh around the room. By the end of that first meeting, I had already made two hundred and forty dollars in profit. Everything is falling into place. Almost too well, I thought.

Another perk that came with selling weed is you always have tons of weed around. And the pricing is far superior. Just don't smoke all your profits. You need to maintain some self-control, or you'll be out of business before you know it. I had no choice in that aspect. If I didn't control myself, I would go hungry.

Those college years were so great; I don't think there are words to fully describe it. I was on top of the world. I finally had an elite group of friends, loads, and heaps of girls around all the time. I am addicted to all of it, pot life, I guess. I went out every night, except for Sundays, to make sure I would never miss a thing—the constant fear of missing out, the FOMO. I needed to be around the action. That insatiable craving brought me many great tales and companions that would last a lifetime. It taught me a valuable lesson about what I was looking for and what I genuinely needed—my tribe.

The gut-wrenching feeling of my last drive out of the Oneonta State University of New York is still palpable to this day. My friends and I always joked about getting older. We would dramatically shout, It's over, dude... all over. Now it was over, and it was devastating. I lit up the last joint and took one last slow ride down the main street, and I got all choked up. Goodbye, my love. Parting was such sweet sorrow.

17

A Moment in Time

I am engaged to Karen, and within a year of that, I marry her in Key West. Good old brother Christian officiated our wedding in style and grace. Suppose you never explored Florida's expansive waterways from a ship. In that case, you may not have lived Florida life to the fullest. Karen and I take my boat from Tampa, down the coast, and down South to the Florida Keys, and cruised up the east coast. Such natural beauty to take in the wildlife, dolphins, and crystal-clear blue-green turquoise water that you could see straight down to the bottom twenty feet or more.

Mortgages are booming with sub-prime loans, no income check, no asset check, one hundred percent financing with a 660-credit score. These banks are brokering shady deals. I am not complaining; these banks are practically giving money away, and the broker is reaping huge payouts. As in so many eras of overindulgence, so many people manipulate the system, this bubble will inevitably pop. Still, I am on the surfboard, riding this wave until it crashes. I determine now that cannabis is genuinely a recession-proof business. When things go well in society, when people are financially comfortable, they will spend money on pot and other entertainment commodities. However, they still spend money on cannabis and other party products when things are going poorly. I love cannabis culture and pot-life, but how can I earn money legitimately this way?

We quickly find and buy our first home in South Tampa, and the full-court pressure on Karen to have kids has intensified. I am getting older now, and I do not want to wait much longer. She continually rejects the idea and says she is not ready for kids, but she finally concedes. We move entirely into our new place together with my Pitbull Peachy, and it makes our house a family home, and I think we are content here. It does not take long for Karen to conceive, and we find out she is having a bouncing baby boy, a boy. I am amazed by the unexpected joy and love I feel. I love him before I even know him; the anticipation is unbelievable. The time leading up to the due date is uncommonly stirring. It has me thinking more than ever about something, someone bigger than me in this world. I am going to be a dad; this is my kid, my boy. I am both amazed and bewildered. Something about a child makes you rethink some of your lifestyle and habits quickly; you wake up, grow up, and realize unconditional love. The mortgage and real estate industries are booming, so my dad and I open a Mortgage-America in Tampa. I figure I will earn money in the lending brokerage business until I can figure out what I want to do. What path will I carve out for my life for my son?

Karen is feeling annoyed with all that comes with pregnancy. Her back and feet hurt every day. Round like a basketball, her belly bulges, and I think she might pop any day now.

It is a brisk, chilly winter day in Florida, even though that only means sixty degrees. I sit up in bed and stretch; I casually look to my side. I usually see the bulge of her belly pushing the sheets up, but she is not in bed this morning. She must have gotten up early for a snack, I assume. I slide my legs out of bed, and my feet touch the cold terrazzo floor. I yawn loudly and stretch while walking toward the restroom and shake off the stiffness I feel; I need coffee.

Feet are shuffling and dragging as I come to the restroom where Karen is standing frozen in stature. She appears terrified or excited; I was not sure.

Baffled, I ask, "What's up? What are you doing? Are you ok?" She hesitates and says, "It's time." Oh shit! Its time. I don't know what sort of force took over my body, but I grab our baby bag lovingly packed in this day's plan and my car keys plus water. The car has a car seat snuggly fit for our newborn already.

"Ok, let's go, be careful, go slow," I reassure her as I hold her arm and support some of her and the baby's weight on mine. She sluggishly steps one foot in front of the other, hand-wrapped under her belly, and a few cringes of grimacing pain are noticeable on her face. I help her in the car seat and shut the door. I haul ass to the driver's seat, start the engine, and head to the hospital. Like a cyclone churning my reality, the rush of everything is exhilarating and nauseating all at the same time. We arrive at the hospital; it is all a blur. Surreal, I usher inside, admitted into the hospital where Karen is ready for this time. I am told by the nurses to wait, and I sit in an uncomfortable chair nearby. I am afraid, and I grip her hand and reassure her all is well. Hours go by, and the doctor comes in to help in the last stage of my son's arrival.

I waited to hear his cry, but I hear the nurses and doctor talking about the cord. I stand to see his body is purple as the doctor gets him free just in time for a quiet cough and sputter, and out comes his scream—the umbilical cord is no longer around his neck. I see the nurse pick him up to show me his thick head of black hair, and my first thought is, this is my kid? Dylan is his name. A moment in time I will always cherish.

18

Black Mamba

The sun shines brilliantly through my kitchen window as I sit to eat a turkey sandwich for lunch; the glare almost blinds me. Dylan is so fussy, but I got him to sleep for a much-needed nap after a big lunch and playing ball in the yard with dad for a little while. Karen is upstairs, and I am stressing about work, and Karen is distant. I think she is often stressing with Dylan, so I help ease the stresses during lunches or at home. I am home more; lately, loans are becoming challenging to find, and when I see them, they are harder to close. I cannot stop thinking about a recent refinance deal went wrong. The bank I used for the sale goes belly up; I did not get paid for my work. I am out of the money, time, and strength to deal with this shit for much longer. I doubt the longevity of my career choice at this point. I am so sick of it; no more getting by and always falling back on cultivating pot. It does not work for my life or family any longer. I am reinventing myself, time for a change; I have had enough.

The loud ring of my cell phone breaks the silence of my deep thought. Oh shit, caller ID reads Vinny. He is one of my old college friends. I pick up and press the accept button and bring it to my ear.

"Hey man, what's up!" I say enthusiastically.

"What's up, man! Ya, so, I just moved to St. Petersburg, right near you, dude!" He declares from the other end of my phone. Vinny is an absolute character who fits right in with mutual friends Dennis and Dena from New York.

"We need to get together, man," I say. I am happy he is calling me to catch up finally.

"Hey, my friend Justin and his wife just moved here from New York, too. We all need to make some money. You know my work, and I can speak for Justin, too."

"You know you're in Vinny, no problem," I assure.

Vinny laughs and says, "Justin is a cool guy; he fits in with us all if you know what I mean. Justin's wife, Jill, is a pediatric doctor; she is pro-medical cannabis. This woman educates me on the health benefits of weed for my anxiety and shit," he laughs loudly. Our group of friends is going to be a gigantic party.

"Wow, that is great. Unreal, but do you see how doctors know these things? Society is just catching up," I surmise and laugh. I hear Dylan crying in the other room. "Hey, I need to let you go; let's catch up later," I genuinely propose.

"Absolutely, man, later," he says as the phone clicks to hang up. I put my phone down and run to pick up my baby. He's three now, but he is still my baby boy. I pick Dylan up from his crib and bring him to play in the living room; he is so darn cute. I smile and kiss him, but all he wants are his toys in the living room. All the bells and whistles on the toys, and he loves playing with them.

* * *

After a few months of working with me, Justin becomes friendly with a man who is doing loans out in Colorado; his name is Jamal. Justin and I have gotten to know each other since Vinny introduced him to me, and he is a cool guy and easygoing. Jamal is a mortgage professional who ultimately turns into a guy searching for the next thing to do with himself like all of us are now. Many in the mortgage industry are trying to switch into commercial loans and find it more challenging to close these. Jamal and Justin work on a possible commercial agreement for weeks, but then it dissolves, and we are all shit out of luck. It is slim pickings for real estate, and we are not the only people struggling.

Months go by with no income from mortgages, and all the while, Jamal continues calling Justin to chat about his friend Chris. Chris is selling some legal pot to smoke shops in Colorado with a lot of success. I have heard about fake weed for years and assume it is just weird looking grass that resembled weed but didn't have any effects. Jamal is so persistent bragging about his friend Chris and how we need to connect with him to do business. We are all getting desperate for cash and agree we will try it if the sample they send us is deserving of anything. I figure that if it is worth a damn, I will be the first to know.

When the package arrives at the doorstep of my house, Karen spots the delivery guy in his brown button-up shirt tucked in his shorts. He gets into his brown box UPS truck to drive away to his next delivery.

Karen shouts, "Package delivered, guys." Vince, Justin, and I are having lunch in my kitchen, just laughing and talking about how the real estate lending market has tanked, and is it worth it to stay in this career? We look at each other, and we immediately know it is the samples from Jamal. Justin and I have been talking about this stuff for a week now since Jamal sent the mysterious legal weed. I get up from my seat excitedly and race down the hall to my front door. I anxiously turn the knob to open the door, and there in front of me on the ground, sitting on my welcome mat, is a small brown box. I bend down to pick it up, step backward inside and close the door. I skip to the kitchen and present the small cardboard box on the table directly in front of Vince.

"It's here, man, let's try this shit," I announce as I reach in my silverware drawer for a knife to cut the thick packaging tape. I draw out a small paring knife from my drawer and gently yet quickly slice through the scotch tape along the box's seam. I pull out all the thick brown packing paper stuffed inside. A single clear plastic jar with a sticker on the side reads Black Mamba (not for human consumption). It looks similar to oregano, I believe. I open the screw-top and examine its contents; I put my nose down on the jar and drew in a deep sniff and scoff. I give the Black Mamba jar to Vince with a perplexed look.

"Doesn't look or smell like a weed," Vince says.

So Justin, Vince, and I sit down at my kitchen table, and I pull out my little blue acrylic water pipe, Mr. Ripley. I pack Mr. Ripley up with the oregano looking herbs and take a hit. I light it up and draw in the harsh smoke; it is brutal. It tastes terrible too. Justin and Vince each take turns. It comes back to me, and I repack it one more time. I take my turn, and it continues around; each of us is making faces of disgust until it dissipates, and then we wait.

I put my head back, close my eyes, and look up at Justin after about a minute and say," I think I am feeling something…" I am feeling a little hazy, also slightly euphoric.

Vince immediately responds, "I feel something, too."

Justin's eyes are turning red, and he states, "Holy shit dude… I'm high right now!"

"Damn, man, this shit is legit; I can't believe it," I yell. I am surprised at the intensity of this feeling in my body.

"I'm out. Wow. And this shit is legal?" Vince questions as he giggles, "How can something that gets you this baked be legal? There's no way."

"Interesting," I suppose. Very interesting. My rollers are turning now; my mind is spinning.

We wait and relax almost an hour for the Black Mamba to wear off, and Justin calls Jamal.

"Jamal, what's up, man? Justin here, yeah, well, we just tried that Black Mamba shit you sent us and, uh. It got us stoned the fuck out!" Vinny and I can hear Jamal laughing through the phone piece, and we look at each other and laugh too.

"We need to set up a conference call with Chris right away," Justin states.

"No problem, guys," Jamal says. "I'm on it." So with that interaction, it passes the test by me with flying colors. The next questions are, what is it, and how is it legal? We do some quick computer research investigation and find out synthetic cannabinoids are an up-and-coming business and an opportunity we do not wish to pass up. Justin wants to know more, just like I do. Vince is out; his wife says she has a bad feeling about it, so he leaves to go back home. Justin and I sit at my kitchen table and call Chris, the Black Mamba herb guy, on speaker.

We introduce ourselves, and I ask, "So what's in this stuff,

Chris, because whatever it is, it worked!"

He laughs, and with a deep raspy baritone voice, he says, "we are infusing these products with a chemical called JWH-018."

"What's that?" Justin questions.

Chris describes, "JWH-018 is the best of the synthetic cannabinoids available. They make it in a laboratory at Clemson University by a Chemist named John W. Huffman, hence the name JWH. I guess his 18th trial is the best."

"So this stuff is legal... Jamal is saying that you are selling it to stores in Colorado and Utah?" I curiously investigate.

"Yep," he says, "I've been hitting all the smoke shops I can find. I'm even selling it at Mom and pop shops, stores that sell Perfume, gas stations, thrift stores, restaurants, you name it. I'll go in anywhere. I make up a bunch of small sample bags and staple them to my business card. A lot of them are calling back, and then we're off to business. If you guys are interested, I can give you Randy's number. He's the one that is manufacturing it."

I hint, "Ok, that would be great. As long as that's ok with you, that's great. Thanks, Chris." He gives me Randy's phone number, and I scribble it on a piece of paper lying in my mail pile on the counter.

I immediately go to my computer in the next room and google JWH-018, and Wikipedia pops up first.

They have synthesized a variety of chemical compounds that affect the endocannabinoid system. JWH-018 is one of these compounds, with studies showing an affinity for the cannabinoid (CB1) receptor five times greater than that of THC. Cannabinoid receptors are in mammalian brain and spleen tissue; however, the active sites' structural details are unknown. Legal status in the USA: Unscheduled. Meaning that it is legal as fuck.

I pick up my phone and dial Chris's contact with Randy, who tells me he lives in Utah. He tells me about how he has made his fortune in Phone Calling cards back in the '90s and is now on the verge of this substantial up-and-coming market. Lucky for me, he is coming to Tampa in a week, and we agree to meet up with him at a hotel near the airport where he is staying. I end my call with Randy, and Justin and I talk for the rest of the day about the possibilities.

Randy is a nice guy. Average clean-cut, well-spoken in his early 50s, I venture. Well-spoken and seems to have his shit together, so that eases my concerns a bit. I wonder if I can do my website for the specific product, he calls Black Mamba, and he says it is terrific. No one else has done anything online yet, so it is all sounding grand. He gives me the whole saga about the merchandise and where it is progressing, and I am unbelievably thrilled.

After the meeting, I go on GoDaddy and buy the domain name BlackMambaShop.com. I have some necessary basic HTML web page building abilities, so I imagine this webpage will be the easiest way to start. I already have a PayPal account, and within six hours, I have a primary site up and running. We only purchased ninety-six of his one-gram jars. He also has three-gram, and on the site, I made it possible for customers to buy up to four grams at a time at a slightly discounted price. I honestly did not imagine there would be much interest. Less than eight hours after the site goes up, a purchase. Four of the four-gram jars. I call Justin to let him know, and he is just as shocked as I am.

"That's a good sign, selling this much on the first day? In the first eight hours," Justin says.

"Hell Yeah, that's a good sign," I reply.

I can not believe it. The hair on the back of my neck is standing straight up. I am super pumped. I think to myself, can I finally quit mortgages? I sure do hope so.

Over the first few months, the sales keep rolling in online, and Justin focuses on face-to-face meetings with any store owner. We copy what Chris taught us by making up a few hundred small sample baggies and stapling them to business cards. Justin is good at not taking no for an answer. He keeps advancing into the shops, and he is making good headway on signing up new stores.

One particular spot he keeps trying is the old historic district of Tampa called Ybor City. We know Ybor City was founded in the 1880s and for its handmade rolled cigars. Starting in the 1980s, it turned into a nightlife area. 7th Avenue is the main street that closes off car traffic on Friday and Saturday nights to accommodate all the area's partiers.

The only Smoke Shop on 7th Ave is a place called Hot Wax. It is right next to the center of town, aptly named Centro Ybor. It is open until three a.m. and frequently has many entertainers. Performers either play at the music venue across the street called Masquerade or go on the main drag to find their way back into the store location and coolness factor hangout. Justin finally gets through to the owner of the Hot Wax shop one afternoon by accident. He is walking in right as two guys were walking out. Justin overheard them talking about the use or nonuse of the word Bong.

"It's Not a Bong…" One guy argues, "It's a water pipe; make sure you never use the word bong." Justin sees an opportunity and steps into the conversation.

"Yeah, I have heard about that before. Didn't the Federal

Government make that word illegal?"

"Yeah, something like that," the man answers.

"My name is Justin. What's up, man?"

"Billy. What's up, dude?" and they shake hands. Justin goes on. "Hey, I see you guys carry some of that pot-pourri. Are you interested in carrying a high-quality product? I've been in a few times to set up a meeting, but I haven't heard from anyone."

"Yeah, man," Billy says. What's the name of yours? We get a ton of samples every day."

"Black Mamba," Justin responds. "We can beat anyone's pricing, and the shit is outstanding. I can drop off some on consignment and see how it goes."

Billy replies, "Maybe we could try it, bring back some product and an invoice, and ask Patty or me. We'll put it out and see how it goes." Justin shakes his hand and says, "Sounds great, man. I'll be back in two hours."

Two minutes later, Justin calls me with the enthusiastic news," Hey, I think I just got us that smoke shop in Ybor I was telling you about, Hot Wax. The owner Billy just told me to bring back some shit to get us started. He's a youthful hippie dude."

"Nice dude," I returned. "So, how many does he want?"

Justin says, "We'll give him two boxes of the 1 gram and 3 grams and see how it goes. It would help if you met him. I think we can get things going down here in Ybor."

I remark, "sounds great. Oh, and we just got another online sale for $179. A bunch of three-gram containers, and I just got another call from a store owner named Mohamed, who wants many ten-gram jars. We need to buy bulk and create our own ten-gram jars. Probably start our brand, too, so we can start making some cash."

"I'm all in," Justin says. "This shit is moving fast. I think we are on to something here, dude. We can barely keep up with the demand already. We need an office, and we need one soon."

"I know," I acknowledge. "My neighbor is giving me dirty looks at the people coming and going… let's look for an office."

19

Hot Wax

J ustin and I determine to move forward with finding the
perfect small office space plus warehouse. We find one
location halfway between our homes; we see what seems
to be the ideal spot, possibly. Close to around two-thousand
square feet, five rooms, it fits our needs well. Together Justin
and I check it out. Walking through the rooms, I can sense this
because this will be our new business site, and we take it. The
rent is cheap, and although not the most beautiful space, it will
do for our increasing needs. The demand has required me to
hire some help for packing and shipping, and this newfound
e-commerce success is up and running. An ad in the Craigslist
and we are plus-four with new employees eager to operate.

Our new bestselling store, Hot Wax, is coming in for its
third wholesale order for Black Mamba spice. We are settling
into the office, and everything is looking magnificent. I am
convening, checking emails on my new desktop when Justin
strolls in my office, talking on the phone. I spin around in my
office chair and look at him; he smiles and nods his head with
a hell-ya gesture. Justin is talking with Billy from Hot Wax

again.

"Yeah, perfect, tomorrow at one o'clock, at the store." He hangs up and starts jumping around like a little kid. "Another order, dude. This time he wants ten boxes of the one-gram and ten boxes of the three grams. He also wants ten-gram jars. I keep telling you about this; we need to do the ten-gram jars ourselves."

"Yes. I'm on it," I say. "I found a local place to get those jars. Let's go there first tomorrow; we can head to Ybor to meet Billy after; Justin, fucking awesome work with him, I am curious to see what he is up to."

"Sounds excellent, thanks," Justin answers.

I spend the rest of the afternoon brainstorming the packaging and label for our product and decide that we will go to the Container Store in the morning and Hot Wax in the afternoon.

I have been to Ybor City at night a bunch of times, but never during the day. It appears to be shabby looking, some trash blowing around, and beggars hitting us up all along the circuit. Justin and I are walking toward the shop, and I feel miserable for these men. An older, very suntanned man sitting on a makeshift mat looks up as I pass and pleads, "Help a disabled Veteran, any spare change?" I walk past and ignore, I do not have change anyway, but I feel sad, which is also a problem for me. I can get snared in thought about how people jump from one extreme to another, from prosperity to poverty, full of passion, and even rebelling against society's status quo. Caught in a moment of reflection, I didn't even realize we have arrived at the storefront. Cool location, a busy spot at night, has an ample front window space and huge double doors. Justin and I walk inside, and it is very spacious and has an inviting sense. The walls have vinyl records, almost wholly covering any visible area. It is outdated, and I am not crazy about the decor. It is not what I was expecting to see.

A clean-cut bearded man walks up with a smile and says, "What's up, guys." Justin and I look up at him. Is this Billy? I wonder.

"Oh, hey, Billy, what's up," Justin says. "Billy, this is my partner Kevin. Kevin, this is Billy, the guy I am telling you about."

Once again, I am surprised. "You're Billy? Hey, how are you, man? Justin tells me you are a hippy type, so I was not expecting you." I shrug and laugh and reach to shake his hand firmly.

Billy laughs and remarks, "Not a hippy, more of a student slash businessman. Just trying to make some money and finish up school."

"What are you majoring in school?" I question.

"Engineering," he replies. "I have around one year left, and I'll finish, I hope."

"Nice. So, you're a smart smoke shop owner, good for you," I quip. He seems relaxed and comfortable to be around.

Billy laughs and declares, "Our buyers keep asking if you have anything new, any new brands or flavors?" We did not have any new flavors; we need more, I decide. We will need to create a new brand; we will need one that says it is a potent product. The most powerful thing possible would be best. We hang out at Hot Wax for approximately twenty more minutes and say our goodbyes. I can sense Billy is intelligent, and he also has an outgoing, confident way about him. I like him, I conclude. We wave, push the doors open, and I pat Justin on the back. We chuckle and agree to meet back at the office; we have some business to do.

I pick up my pace toward my car, and I notice the concrete landscape as I step along the way. Many young people are sitting, hanging out; there is a mix of all ranges and diversity; no wonder the product is flying off the shelf. Young people are more open to cannabis culture than my generation; the 'Just Say No' eighties campaign, the stigma era. Maybe one day, decriminalization, and normalization? I use it for my anxiety; it helps a lot.

I find my car, open the door, and go back to the office where Justin is waiting. Like lightning, it hits me. I practically audibly hear the words, dead man, walking. Oh my god, the brand name, this is it, it is perfect; where do I come up with this shit sometimes? It must be the cannabis talking to me, Mary Jane, my muse. I laugh as I step out of my car; I am excited to tell Justin my idea as I march toward the front office. I go straight over to my office, where Justin waits. I ask him to stay that I need to look something up online before we discuss it.

"I have an idea for the brand," I declare and light up like a lightbulb. I sit in my chair and spin around to my desktop. I google the name Dead Man Walking and then find a T-shirt for weddings or bachelor parties with this little generic skeleton art walking along. I immediately copy and paste it and make our label, just like that. It looks hilarious. I spin back around and proudly present to Justin the computer screen's display, our new brand, our new label, Dead Man Walking.

With a new name, Justin and I figure we need a new, more potent product. Maybe with a little unique flavor, so I call up Randy from Black Mamba. He tells me he can make a loose herb product for me at a much more favorable price. He does his magic potency boost and adds little spearmint herbs to the mix, and that is all we need. Dead Man is an instant success.

107

Our sales double again over the next two months.

At Hot Wax again, we drop off more products and grab a cold beer when we see Billy. Before we head out for a cold one, Billy waves for us to come over to him. He points at the pot-pourri display cabinet.

"Check this out. Empty again, that Dead Man Walking shit is killing it right now. Are you guys making it?"

"No," I laugh. "I wouldn't even know where to start with that. We're just buying it from our supplier." I explain.

"I might help you with that," he says. I bet I can make that shit easy."

I tell him confidently, "If you can make it, I'll buy it. If it is effective, that is."

"Oh, it will work," he acknowledges. "Don't worry about that."

We shake on it, and honestly, I didn't even really think about it again until around a week later. Billy shows up at our warehouse and throws a bag on my desk.

"Here you go," he states. "I messed around with the formula a little. Did a few tests run and came up with this? It's a Damiana herb mix with JWH-018. I also made up some separate batches with JWH-020 and another batch with one called AM-2201. I'm still working a bit with those, but we can start with 018."

"Nice," I respond, "That is fast work. You made it yourself?"

"So easy," Billy returns.

I say, "I guess I have to try this stuff. Hey, Terry, come in here.

In her mid-fifties, Terry, a recent hire, hippy-type, walks in and says, "What's up?" She looks at me over her glasses and graying hair and smiles.

"Roll me a joint of this stuff, please," I ask politely and hand her the bag. "We need to try some of Billy's new concoction he has just created.

"No problem," Terry shouts and gestures with a salute at the end.

Billy sits down and gets comfortable just as she comes trotting back in with a nice fatty. "Here you go, sir," she says, then turns to go back into the warehouse. I place the joint, draw out my lighter, and I light it up. I take in a big puff and start coughing because the shit savors like crap. We pass it around a few times and wait. I didn't have to wait very long.

"Yep, I'm baked. I think I fancy this high better than weed!" I report.

Billy replies, "CB1 receptors in the brain show five times greater reception to 018 than to THC."

I laugh, "Ok, well, I do not understand what the hell you're talking about, but the high is great. So, we need to talk more. What are you going to charge us for this? If you can beat the price from the other supplier, then we can get things going."

"I don't know yet," Billy says. "Let me crunch the numbers, and we can meet up again soon to discuss." I can see his brain processing as he turns to leave.

"Ok, sounds good. Don't wait too long, though. I'm curious," I return. Billy leaves, and Justin and I slightly smile at each other.

"Let's see what he says," Justin remarks. "Either way, we have around twenty more website orders to pack up for shipping today. You want to help, or should Terry do it?"

I reply, "Terry can do it."

Two days later, Billy is back. We are all busy packing and creating shipping labels. He walks in and says, "What's up, guys. Are you free? Let's talk." He waives his arm as if to say come this way toward the office. Justin and I walk into our office and close the door where Billy is sitting already.

Billy begins, "So I've been thinking. You guys seem to do pretty well these days, and I can make this shit and help with distribution, so what do you guys think about forming a partnership?"

Justin and I look at each other for a moment. "Yeah, we're open to anything, Billy," Justin responds. "How do you see the partnership working?"

I say, "Yeah, I'm interested."

Billy starts his pitch and says, "Well, I paid one hundred thousand dollars for Hot Wax. If you guys were to pay me thirty thousand dollars, we could be equal thirty-three percent partners in the store and of the Pot-pourri company. So, for thirty thousand dollars, you get two-thirds of an established business. I get one-third of a short-term business because we all know what's eventually happening with pot-pourri. That company has a limited lifespan."

I say, "I know Justin and I will both love owning Hot Wax. That I can tell you, it's all exciting. I guess he and I will talk about it a bit and let you know."

I am calm on the outside, but I jump up and down on the inside. Justin and I both know that this whole pot-pourri thing would end eventually, and being partners in an actual store is super exciting.

We leave and go home, and all I think about is Hot Wax. I feel the same feeling; the excitement I had when I was a kid at *the OBI*; the sense of exhilaration this experience is giving me at this moment is extraordinary. I lay my head to sleep, and I think about the cool people I will meet at Hot Wax, and I can finally say I am a business owner. No more bullshit. We will make it the most insanely popular smoke shop in Ybor City. Is this how I can embrace who I am, be genuine, avoid cannabis culture labels, and have a social life?

In the morning, I call Billy and say, "We're in, dude; let's start making some actual money now!" We agree, and it is. The feeling is fabulous, and I spend the day fantasizing about how we are going to increase sales and even redecorate. We are creating cannabis culture here. It is our chance to live our best lives.

We all meet up at Hot Wax and celebrate with a fresh way to get stoned called dabs. Billy tells us that dabs are THC concentrate, around eighty percent as they are referring to. It looks like sticky orange wax. You heat a metal object with a torch and then dab the concentrate on the banger, as they name it, and draw in all the vapor through a water pipe or straw. I am having my dabs with a water pipe, now. That first glob, I slowly put on my banger and then light and inhale, my ears instantly whistle, and I feel the burn in my chest, with an exhale, I am unbelievably high. Mary, is that you? It must be the cannabis talking to me. What resembles a subtle internal voice in my head, I hear the question. Are you high? Do you think they know? An inner dialogue begins. I don't know, do they know, wait, do they even care? I laugh out loud and sit at my computer and act like I am busy, but I'm so high. Does everyone know?

No, everyone else is quiet; they're all as high as you are, relax. This conversation with cannabis goes on in my head for thirty minutes, comical.

20

Safety Meetings

Justin and I are progressing nicely in our new business with our new companies, a great new warehouse, and a new partner, Billy. He is legit. Sometimes in life, there are people, or should I say most of the time, people talk a great game but have no substance to back up their talk. They tell you how great things will be and tell you how much business they're advancing, but never follow through with what they say. Billy is not that person. Every day when I come into work, he is already there. When I leave in the afternoon, Billy will still stay later. When something needs doing immediately or gets postponed at night or on the weekends, he will volunteer. He understands that Justin and I have young kids, so he has no problem stepping up and filling in.

We have the locations; we have the team, and we have the merchandise. There is nothing that can stop us now, like the Chicago Bulls of the 90s. We are getting calls from large distributors all over the country asking for our product. Along with increased sales comes increased profit margins. When you're buying three thousand pounds of Damiana, you are getting it much cheaper than if you purchase less quantity. Jars, labels, and so on are much less expensive this way. We are growing so fast we require a massive warehouse, so we quickly snatch up a place near Hot Wax in Ybor City. Our current space is no longer adequate.

Switching warehouses is a quick and painless process, especially since our warehouse and store sites are in Ybor City nearby each other. We hear rumors from customers and do some internet research about certain chemicals that Florida is banning soon. JWH-018 is at the top of the DEA list of *drugs of concern* or substances that will ban first.

We agree that Florida will ban many of these synthetic cannabinoids; we should move our operation to another state where the law is in our favor. Justin and I are from New York, a State where no potential legislation is coming on any of the synthetic cannabinoids that we are using. It is entirely legal for now.

I call my parents and ask my dad if he knows of any suitable warehouses on Long Island to fit our size and price. He returns with a place in Bayshore that has several spaces for lease. I fly up the following week and meet with the leasing agent and look at a few spots. One of the warehouse spaces he has available is just right; it is the one.

I fly back home immediately, convey my findings, and critique it with the tribe. We all agree it is time to move the business operations to New York, at least partially. There is a lot of activity ahead, and we are all apprehensive about this move, but with all the funds coming in, we know we do not want to rest, not yet at least.

The tribe packs up all our supplies in a few additional vehicles plus a trailer we just purchased—we drive up Interstate

95 to New York. I rent out one of my parents' apartments to live in while I am working. Like in Tampa, I put some job ads on Craigslist, and within a week, our new place is up and running. I can't believe, a year ago, we were scraping along with little of anything going on, and now we are drawing in over a half a million dollars a month.

The saying goes, with more money comes more problems. And with the new location in New York comes additional responsibilities and, well, issues. Justin, Billy, and I develop a plan that the three of us will take turns flying up each week. Luckily for us, there is a direct flight on Southwest Airlines from Tampa to Long Island MacArthur Airport. Every Monday morning, one of us flies up and then comes back on Thursday night. Every time each of us comes in, we are ready to party. With so much money coming in, it is easy to fall into all the bad habits and develop new ones, too. I wind up spending thousands of dollars every time I go; it is my week to spoil myself and the employees. It is all just too much fun not to share the wealth.

We all go out to eat at a restaurant of our choosing, and I always pay the tab gracefully. At the bars and clubs, drinks flow, and I still happily sign the check. For the first time in my life, money is no object. If I want something, I can gain it and not even speculate about it. It feels valid, fulfilling. I think I relish living authentic and contributing to others when I can; it enriches my journey to give.

Our Hot Wax Glass smoke shop in Ybor City is a business we call home. Friday night, we are standing out in front, admiring the tall corner window outside the storefront. In the corner window, sitting for everyone to observe, is Chad Piece, our new glassblower weekend display. He is delicately crafting a one-of-a-kind octopus' glass pipe for everyone to behold. Barehanded and holding a torch, it seems enchanting. People are stopping to observe and crowding around to view the spectacular finish.

A sizeable new restaurant has recently reopened directly next to us called *Carne*, which is glorious news. *Carne* has $2 Finlandia Vodka drinks. With all this money coming in, we are partying non-stop.

Standing outside, mesmerized by the fiery blaze, Billy yells, "*Safety Meeting!*" We call our *Safety Meetings,* which is code for doing cocaine lines in the store's back. Billy marches inside; one by one, we all follow in sequence.

"Yes, yes. Safety is important. Yes, Safety, Safety." We are chuckling and obnoxiously rambling as we make our way.

"You never can be too safe..." Billy replies as we all pile in the back room. Billy is a conscientious worker but can party with the best of us. One by one, we all rip a few more lines, and it is time to head back next door to meet up with our employee Justin's mom. Her boyfriend Bobby "The Chief" Taylor, an NHL goalie for many years, did the color commentating for the Tampa Bay Lightning television broadcasts.

We meet them at the bar and continue with our fun. Employee Justin's mom and The Chief are already drinking martinis.

Justin's mom remarks, "Hey, guys. How's it going? Billy, where is my weed you promised me? I'm completely out. You can't leave me hanging like this."

"It's coming; it's coming. Don't worry. The weed guy is to be here in thirty minutes. So, enjoy yourself, and it will be here before you know it."

Chief says, "How's it going, Billy, Kevin. Good to see you again. Business is still booming, I guess? I hear some stuff from

Justin. It sounds like things are taking off. I thought maybe you could give my son a job?"

"Yes." Billy says, "Tell him to call me."

"Thanks, I'll let him know. He needs to do something. And please hurry and get that pot, would you? She's driving me crazy! Where's Billy, where's Billy, she repeats?"

Billy laughs saying, "Yeah, I'm on it. Not to worry."

Just then, Justin, the partner, and Vince walk over. Vince always makes this crazy sounding Sheep *Baaaaaa* sound.

"What the hell is that?" Chief asks.

"Oh, that's just Vinny. You get used to him," I say with a chuckle.

Worker Justin walks over to us and says, "Billy, can you please get my mom her weed, dude? She's annoying the hell out of me over there, and I don't want to listen to it."

I mention to Billy, asking, "Hey, did you tell Justin about the Condo?"

"What? Condo? Where? Tell me!" Worker Justin asks eagerly.

"Yeah, we're going to buy that condo with a boat slip on Treasure Island, Gulf Coast of Florida."

Suddenly Justin makes a strange face and mumbles through his teeth, saying, "Don't look now, but there's mom's old boyfriend, Scott." We immediately turn to look.

"Guys, I said don't look. You could have been a little more discreet about it. Hey, Scott, what's up?" Justin waves at Scott, and he waves back over to us.

"What do you care if Scott sees us?" I ask. "He's an ex of your Mom."

"Scotts a bit of a badass. He works for the ATF, *the Bureau of Alcohol, Tobacco, and Firearms,* so I don't want him coming over and overhearing about what we're doing. Just look away."

"Sounds like the perfect time for another safety meeting!" Billy shouts.

"Another safety meeting. Did I miss out on one? I need to get up to speed on our company's safety standards."

We all file out of the bar and head back next door to Hot Wax's back room. Once again, lining up and then Vince kept looking at his phone and then yells out.

"Oh my god, Kelly is a huge annoyance right now. I have to go." Vinny reluctantly leaves, going out the back door.

When we walk out the front of Hot Wax onto 7th Avenue, Vince is driving by, and then he slows to a crawl. He rolls down his window as he drives by and then belts out a super loud sheep call," *Meeee-Awwwww, Baaaaaaaaaaa.*" He then peels out, screeching as he drives away.

"What a clown," Billy laughs. We all join in laughing—just another day of the large life in Ybor City.

With all three of us weekly flying back and forth, Billy volunteers for an extra flight; he does not have kids and has a little free time.

21

TSA

Billy has been striving to get fresh sales leads; he is always online, on his phone, and never stops. Stan, a brand-new industry contact, invites Billy to fly to Louisiana to meet with some new players. Jay, Lloyd, Johnny, Lou, and others are from a company named *Peculiar Wares*. They are looking for a new ally to manufacture goods and become partners. Billy kills two birds with one stone. First, he will visit Lafayette, Louisiana, and then jet-set to meet with Ken, a longtime customer who pays in cash.

Upon arriving in Louisiana, Billy goes out with everyone, drinking and socializing all evening. They go to one of the big player's mansion and are having a great time letting loose. On tall wooden bar stools, they sit around laughing, drinking, and getting to know each other. Lloyd is talking to Billy and gradually reveals a story.

"We have so much influence in the state of Louisiana," Lloyd pompously declares. "We have a letter from the Louisiana Attorney General's office. It allows us to sell our product for up to two years; Billy, we need to partner, man," laughs Lloyd.

The *Peculiar Wares* guy glance at each other and shake their heads in agreement with Lloyd. Billy shrugs and takes a sip of his frothy beer.

Lloyd told his story about when he had driven into a statue out front of the town hall in Lafayette, Louisiana, after leaving the pub one night. The cops arrived on the scene. Because of their connections with public officials, the police escorted Lloyd homeward instead of throwing him in jail.

Setting his pint down on the bar top again, Billy says, "Support us in obtaining a letter from the Florida Attorney General, and we are extremely interested in a partnership."

Lloyd looks up at Billy with an intoxicated smirk. He responds, "Some of our *Peculiar Wares* stores we have been selling fifty-thousand dollars a day in spice." Lloyd winks and laughs with the guys. In deep thought, Billy silently crunches the figures. He is hopeful of this new opportunity presenting and enjoys the new company. After a long night of partying, Billy continues to his hotel and passes out.

He wakes up in his hotel bed, hungover. Nothing a good cup-o-joe can't fix. He washes up, packs up, and gets on a plane to Tri-City's airport to convene with Ken for his planned cash transaction.

Billy travels to his next stop, Ken. Completely sold out of their product in Tennessee, Ken anxiously expects Billy's arrival. The neighboring states settle their wholesale orders in cash only. Usually every month, Billy flies in, grabs a duffel bag of bills, and seamlessly flies back home. The system works adequately, but Billy needed an extra few weeks for some personal affairs before going again this time. The payout will be more significant because of the time that has passed.

Ken meets Billy at the airport with the same routine, and

they drive to his warehouse to do the exchange. After walking through the warehouse's broad expanse toward the back office, Billy relaxes in his usual spot. Ken shuffles over to the rear of a ledge, opens a hidden safe, pulls out many large stack bills, and places them on his desk in front of Billy one by one.

Billy states, "Whoa, what is all this? How much do you think you owe me? It is $38,750."

Ken promptly replies, "Yeah, it is. I have some large bills, but this time, small is all I have. Sorry, man."

Billy takes a deep breath, sits back in his chair, and says, "Dude, I have to get on a plane in three hours with all these stacks of bills. Holy shit."

"I'm sorry, man," Ken says. "I wish I had some larger bills, but this store in Memphis gave me so many smaller bills. He's owed me for months. I had to take it. I have some killer nugs for you, though. Here, get a whiff of these bad boys." He proudly shows Billy the herb and points toward a few rolled joints on his pencil holder's side, and shrugs with a suggestive smile.

Billy tilts his head in disappointment and gives Ken a look and says, "I have to get on a plane, Dude, so I cannot take the nugs, but I'll take one of those joints, though. Light it up!"

After smoking the joint, Billy calls TSA to confirm it is acceptable to carry large amounts of cash on the aircraft. TSA maintains that he may carry up to one hundred thousand US dollars domestically. Hence, a quick stop at Ken's favorite barbeque and then back to the airport. Billy shakes Ken's hand steps out of the car and strolls into the airport; his duffle bag is sagging with the bills' weight.

He walks over to the gate, places his roller bag, and loaded duffle bag on the scanner, and the Tri-City TSA agent sees it roll through the scanner filled with stacks of bills, looks up, and lets the bag through. The next agent then hands Billy a clipboard and asks him to fill out a record to declare the cash—no serious issues. He fills it in and boards first-class, relaxes, sleeps, and arouses when the plane is landing for a layover in Atlanta.

As Billy is walking off the ramp to exit the aircraft, his cell phone rings repeatedly. Billy reaches for it to answer. He draws it up to his front to see, and the caller ID says it's Stan.

He clicks to answer, and cheerfully responds, "Hey!"

"Hey man, bad news, cops arrested the *Peculiar Wares* guys for selling AM 2201 and also charged them with bribing public officials," Stan nervously states.

Billy stops walking and shouts, "Holy shit, man! Let me call Kevin immediately. I'll call you back." He hangs up and frantically searches his phone for Kevin's contact information and clicks. No answer. He tries Justin, and he thankfully picks up. Justin is suspicious and suggests Billy get a rental car to drive back the rest of the way. He cannot decide if he should catch the flight now or drive a rental car. Billy considers an arrest, and coincidentally how TSA noticed the cash on the scanner. He feels nervous. Is there any connection? Still, honestly, Billy thinks it will be too exhausting to travel in a vehicle and recommences the flight.

Subsequently landing at Tampa International Airport, approaching the tarmac, four homeland security officials proceed to Billy. Two in the rear and two in front. They grab his arms quickly and notify him that an agent at Tri-City's airport called to inform them that a passenger had traveled with a sizeable amount of cash. They have a few questions. The agents usher him into a room with one table and two chairs and gestures for him to sit and remain.

Agent one remarks, "Nice Rolex, buddy."

They laugh together as Billy sits down in one of the metal chairs. They turn and walk toward separate corners in the room to await additional agents' arrival. After an unknown amount of time passes silently, the door suddenly opens as two men walk into the fluorescent-lit private room.

One agent sits in the remaining metal chair and remarks, "Our dogs tagged your bag for drugs." He sets down his papers on the table and rifles through paperwork as he looks up at Billy.

Billy responds, "There are no drugs in my bag. Not sure why the dogs would tag it." He crosses his arms and sits back in the chair.

Agent two glances at Billy, tilts his head slightly up, and asks," So, where are you headed?"

"I'm heading here, home," Billy says. "Tampa is where I live, where my businesses are." Never has this happened before, and they perplex Billy with the level of interrogation.

Agent one looks down at his notebook and says, "Your marijuana businesses? I see here you have prior arrests for distribution." He turns several paper corners before looking up to scrutinize.

Billy responds, "Yes, a long time ago, but I don't sell marijuana. I sell legal products in my store. We've done over four million in sales this year already. That's why I am here. I pick up my customer's cash payment. I fly back home." He feels highly agitated after waiting so long, only being met with interrogation this way.

Billy demands, "My fiancé is waiting for me. She must get to work in a few hours. I want my bag and money now, please."

Agent two yells out, "Not happening, buddy. The dog hit

your bag, so it is ours now."

Billy shouts back, "Fuck you, man! That money is the proceeds from a legal transaction."

Agent one yells back and leans in to say, "Well, that money is ours now, man. If you try to get a lawyer to fight it, we will expose your business and its illegal dealings with pot-pourri; try us. We know who you are, Billy." The agent threateningly glares.

Billy snaps back and says, "You guys need to get laid," then leans forward and asks, "Am I arrested, or not?" The agents stand up and laugh before walking toward the door.

"You're free to go now. Have a good one!" Agent one responds as they both leave the room.

Billy yells back," Yeah, great; you take my money, my fiancé has been waiting for hours. You guys are dicks!" The door slams in his face. Finally, free to go, he marches out of the room and airport at approximately three in the morning. Kelly waits anxiously outside the airport; she sees him and runs to greet and hug him. They get in the car together, and she has a fat blunt ready, same as every other trip before. He grabs it and instantly lights it up. Kelly scolds him for being so bold.

She yells, "You just got in trouble for all this stuff, and now you are lighting up right outside the building? At least fucking wait until we get on the highway. Oh, my god!" She puts the car in drive and pulls away from the pickup curb just as Billy blows a massive cloud of smoke out the window.

Billy says," No! Fuck them!"

Losing all that cash and Billy getting harassed isn't fun for any of us. We are making so much money, though; we have other things to keep our focus on now. Fighting TSA in court is the last thing any of us want to do. We let the money go; we did not want the pot stirred anymore. No pun intended. Coming up in August 2011 out in Vegas is an industry convention show called *Champs*. The most incredible opportunity to meet all the industry players and hopefully get some new business. The three of us book our tickets and get ready to fly to Vegas for some fun.

22

Vegas

The most revolutionary counter-culture business-to-business trade show of its kind since 1999, Las Vegas, Nevada. *CHAMPS Trade Shows* has been an exhibition of a who's who of the smoke shop culture shift. Thousands of attendees from the wholesale, retail, online, and in-person spaces of this business world, this giant convention has such a variety of people from all walks of life. There are even live glass blowing contests for cash prizes. Unlike mainstream society, the personalities here are among society's fringes. Many choose a different life path with different values rejecting and opposing mainstream—this kind of transformation I see daily. At Hot Wax, the demand for spice and alternative products increases exponentially. The more I see, the more I see a movement that can provoke fundamental human and cultural change around this alternative way of being.

Justin, Billy, and I are just landing in Vegas to attend this memorable occasion. I cannot shake this popular new song playing in my head. Everywhere we go, on the radio, in the club, even at the ball game, it's *The Party Rock Anthem* by LMFAO.

Every day I'm shuffling, shuffling, party rock is in the house tonight, woo! Everybody just has a good time, hey! Shuffling, shuffling.

We are staying at the Aria Suites, a gorgeous and contemporary, stylish hotel; our suites have panoramic views overlooking the strip. We check in around eleven p.m. and party on the strip all night. The next morning is a little tough to wake up, but with a coffee from the reception, we are off on a mission to grab some breakfast and walk over to the convention center to check in at *CHAMPS*. We eat what we can in the hotel restaurant and walk to the show. Walking toward the check-in area, we notice that most exhibitors are selling spice—one after the next selling their, *not for human consumption* pot-pourri.

I am amazed at all the stalls, various smoking papers, glass water pipes, cleaning products for your smoking piece, and hot trade show models. This place has it all; I turn to see an engaging booth called Jack's Magic Beans. I walk toward the booth curiously, and a man in a fancy suit in his thirties comes toward me.

"Would you like to try some of our magic beans? Here, try one of our samples." He insists and hands me a black sample packet with a bean logo on it.

I smile and reach for the small square packet. I inspect the packaging, the art, and label; it reads **Plant Fertilizer. Not for human consumption**.

I look up at him and ask, "Is this mephedrone?" I have read about this research chemical online; some customers ask about this in Hot Wax and say it is euphoric energy.

"I'm not saying it is, and I'm not saying it's not," he declares with a wink.

With a raised eyebrow, I look back at Justin; he laughs and

shrugs.

"I hear they call it *meow-meow*. Give me a few more of those, please; I've heard good things," I reveal as I stuff a few squares in my pocket. Justin immediately grabs a few as well and fills his pocket.

Then, another guy in a fancy suit walks over and says, "We're having a special party in the Real-World Suite at the Palms. You guys should come." He hands us an invitation, and we shake hands.

"The Real-World Suite, that's at The Palms, right?" Justin asks.

"Yes, it is; I'm Alex. You guys should come; we have a nice setup; bring some ladies if possible," he says.

"I'm Kevin; what's up, Alex?" I question. "What time?"

Alex shakes my hand again and says, "after ten, nice meeting you guys. Maybe I'll see you later. Have a good show, and try those samples."

There is so much pot-pourri, new giant vaporizer contraptions, wild berry incense, a redhead straddling a pole on a sign. Wait, what? The sign reads **Big Pipe**. I laugh; I'll go check this place out. I stroll over to the booth and notice it is all metal pipes. They have different colors and styles and an excellent big display with the lines all strapped in. I am looking through the case and admiring the pieces when a man hands me a flyer; I stop to look at the brochure and read about some events going on. Suddenly I hear a girl moaning softly. I look up and around but see no one. I listen to it again and keep looking around back and forth, and just then, from under the table, a girl pops her head out from under the tablecloth.

She staggers toward me with a deep southern draw, declaring, "Shit, it fucked me up last night." She naturally puts her hands on my shoulder and asks, "Hey, honey, how are you doing?" She smiles with striking, bright blue eyes. Ash brown hair pulls back into a bun, revealing her sassiness.

I am surprised at her charm and answer, "Doing good. I'm good. I guess nap time is over?" I question and beam.

"Shit yeah, naps over. And that felt good, too; I needed that. Well, I need to head to the ladies' room. See you around, guys." She yells over to the guy at the booth, saying, "I'll be back in five Cliff."

"All right," Cliff yells back from inside the booth.

As she walks away in her t-shirt and crop jean shorts, I notice that she is hot.

"Wow," I mutter under my breath and glance back until she is out of view.

We need to meet up with our new chemical suppliers, Johnny, and Lou. All we need to do is follow the sound of the *Party Rock Anthem*. We make our way over, and there they are, two guys in all their spray-tanned glory ripped jeans with chains, standing at the booth in between two promo models doing their best booty shaking. These guys are characters. Everything about them is over the top. They have huge speakers blaring beats; strippers flew out from Atlanta to hang out with them and booty shake around their booth. They have money, an obvious fact.

Billy walks up first, and then one guy shakes my hand and screams over the loud music.

"Hey, what's up, man? I'm Johnny," he yells and reaches to shake my hand.

I shake his hand back firmly and say, "What's up? I'm Kevin. Good to meet you," I say with my best tough-guy voice.

Johnny says, "You're Billy's partner? Nice to meet you. So,

our guy Stan here is telling us you guys are ready to buy some quantity?"

"Yes, we were looking to get fifty keys or kilos to start," I respond. "If the price works, we would want more. Up to a hundred a month. We're growing fast right now."

"Nice man, nice," Johnny says back. "Well, I know Stan has something planned for a little later on today, and tonight we are going to get fucked up, bro!" He has a drink in one hand and grabs me around my neck with his other. "Tonight, I'm going to hit Vegas like a fucking champ, and then I'm going to fuck four bitches at once." He points over to the group of booty shakers, shaking their booties to-and-fro.

He continues saying, "Tomorrow, we can talk more about products correctly."

"That sounds great," I say. I nod my head and agree with him.

"I have to take a piss. Have a good one, guys," Johnny says as he releases me from his grasp and starts walking away.

I get a bit of a negative feeling about this arrangement. These guys are way too out in the open about everything. Too flashy and boisterous. I immediately start thinking this is precisely the thing I would not be doing. Overdone at a trade show is not how I will act if I sell millions of dollars in marginally legal research chemicals.

My stomach is churning. I notice our new friend Stan that Billy met in Lafayette, Louisiana, walks up to us.

"Hey guys," Stan says as he shakes our hands one at a time. "How's it going? I guess you met Johnny and Lou already?"

"Yes, we just did," I say with a bit of a glare.

Stan says, "A little later, we're having a meeting with some industry's big players to discuss how we can organize and get proper legal representation. It's called the PGA, Peculiar

Goods Association."

Billy jumps in and says, "Yeah, I had told Justin and Kevin about that. It sounds like a good idea to stay on top of this cat-and-mouse industry we're in."

Stan continues, "Yes, the idea is for all of our members to have the most up-to-date information to focus on how to sell and market their products. One of the prominent marijuana attorneys will be there. You guys should come over. Here's the information. It starts at 8."

Billy says, "Yes, we're all going to go. Are Lloyd and Jay going to make it?"

"No, they don't land until eleven. We'll meet up together tomorrow." The speakers blast *They Know* by Drake, and all the stripper chicks shake their butts, spinning, and twirling.

Stan smiles and laughs, "Alright, guys, see you later, have fun."

As we all walk away from the blasting music, I ask Billy, "Lloyd and Jay? Who are they?"

Billy says, "Yeah, Lloyd and Jay are from the business named *Peculiar Wares*. They own twenty-something stores in Louisiana and Georgia. They have been looking for a new manufacturer of loose products. After getting arrested, they say all charges are being dropped if they find a new compliant pot-pourri formula to stay legal and stay in business. That would be us. Stan and I know them, and it sounds like an excellent opportunity."

Justin quickly says, "Fuck yeah, and the loose product is so much easier than doing all that packaging crap. Just put it in garbage bags and ship it out."

By this point, I am utterly exhausted, but there is no time to rest. Justin, Billy, and I all head back to clean up at the hotel.

Hopefully, eat something, re-energize, and then get ready for round two tonight.

23

Big Pipe

Advancing in our cab up to the front of the hotel Aria, the taxi operator shimmies the automobile under the lobby, over-passing and pushing the brakes. Billy and I are getting out while Justin is paying the driver in cash. As I step out of the yellow car, I look up and around, soaking in all the lights and sounds, the hustle and bustle of hotel attendants, valet drivers rushing. I love the energy and feeling I get when I am in Vegas. Justin finishes paying and hurries outside of the car to join us; we aim and walk toward the hotel's lobby entrance. We pass through the automatic double doors and step inside, look at one another, and agree to meet back up in the lobby around five.

The conference Stan scheduled for us is about discovering and gaining some much-needed legal advice about spice or pot-pourri. It is a synthetic cannabinoid; we need a thorough understanding of the legality.

After the meeting concludes, I casually wave to the guys and make my way toward the elevator. I need a snooze to be decent for the rest of what will probably be a long night. I am half asleep by the time I practically portal instantly to our room. My body drops onto my bed as the door closes behind me; I sink in on my super plush cozy mattress, kick my shoes off, and bury my face in my down-filled pillow, lights out.

After my restful nap, I shower, call Karen, and make sure she, Dylan, and my newest Jacob are okay. Jacob just turned one, and I want to make sure they are okay. All is well to go out tonight, and I am thrilled. As I am leaving, I remember Jack's Magic Bean samples in my jeans. I grab the jeans, reach in the side, and pull out the black bean packets. Ding! Tonight, will be magical. I grin and shove the packs in my pocket, imagining the next party and the fun we will have, but first, the conference. We meet in the lobby, grab a quick bite to eat, and we are back outside to flag down a cab.

Justin gets one right away, runs over, and states, "We need to go to El Cortez." The cab driver gestures to get in, and we simultaneously walk around and get inside.

"Okay, that's around 15 minutes away," declares the driver.

"Why so far away?" I ask.

"Stan says he reserved a conference room over there for this PGA meeting," Billy says. The cab driver confirms and drives away to our destination.

"This will be good if we get some legal advice; we can plan out how these substances are going to be handling. Stan also says we need a Florida attorney who can write us a letter confirming legal business action. It could be an enormous benefit to us down the road in case there are any legal problems. The lawyer's name Stan gave me is attorney Jim D. Once we get back home to Tampa, I will call him," I say.

We get to El Cortez and eventually locate the room where the conference is going on. We see a lot of the same guys from the trade show event. Everyone gathers around in a half-circle, and Stan steps up to speak.

"Thanks for coming here tonight. I know most of you want to keep this short and sweet to get back to Vegas as soon as possible. I just wanted to get this group together to talk about what the PGA can do to help you plan for what is coming. Everyone knows that the list of chemical compounds that the states are banning is growing by the day. We've brought in our legal specialist to represent our industry and break down a state-by-state detailed list of what you can and cannot sell in each state. As the substances get banned, to stay in business, you will need new and legal chemicals. We can help with all of that."

Stan goes on and on for another ten minutes. Then, some groups of people explain their situations. I never utter a word. I am always afraid to be on the front lines of this pot-pourri industry. I do not want to be the industry's face, and I do not wish anyone to know who I am. So after another thirty minutes of hiding in plain sight, the meeting is thankfully over. I am one of the first ones out the door.

"What do you guys think?" Justin asks once we make our way to the lobby.

"I think we need to speak with that attorney, Jim D," I reply.

Billy responds, "okay, you call him, and I will see if I can get a copy of that state-by-state list from Stan. We should have that list if we are going to continue shipping this shit all over the country."

I take a deep breath and say, "Okay, so enough business talk, let's head over to that early party at the Hard Rock."

"Yes, let's," says Justin.

Another cab ride and we are at the Hard Rock. Randy, our

supplier from Black Mamba, has a side party. He has a bowling alley inside his hotel suite. We ride up the elevator to the entertainment floor. I knock on the door, and a cute girl opens the door, greets us right away, and ushers us inside.

"Come on in," she says.

The place looks like the early eighty's decor at its finest. A live DJ and the bowling alley are fully functional. We all grab a free drink and scan the scene; it is probably too early for any real party action. I look at the two of them, and we agree that it is time to leave.

Five minutes later, we are back down in the Hard Rock lobby, and we head for the Center Bar in the casino. As we're making our way through the maze of slot machines and blackjack tables, the song Party Rockers plays. This song plays everywhere, all the time; I laugh, and suddenly remember my Jack's magic beans in my pocket; I pull out the package between my two fingers and hold it up.

"Guys, guys, wait," I say as I stop and rest on a bar stool nearby. I hold the pack up so Justin and Billy can see. With my suggestive head tilt and a questioning shoulder shrug, we all laugh.

Out of nowhere, someone hastily snatches the small pack out of my hand and says with a southern draw, "Oh yeah, I saw this shit at the booth near us." I turn around, and it is the big pipe girl that had crawled out from under the table at the trade show. She's the one who grabs it from my hand.

I snatch it back from her and reply, "Hey, give me those beans." We laugh, and she hands it back to me.

"I've tried that faux co, you know, fake coke, before," she replies. "Not Jack's beans, something named Ivory Wave. That shit kept me up for days," she declares. She is so attractive and

135

relaxed, very confident when she speaks; it is impressive. The tight t-shirt and jeans get me every time.

"So, we've never officially met," I say. "I'm Kevin. and you are...?"

"Kat," she says. "Nice to meet you, Kevin."

She points to her left and says, "This is my friend Jen." Two beautiful women and the nighttime is off to a magnificent commencement.

"Hey, Kat and Jen, this is Justin and Billy, my business partners. Guys, this is the girl I was telling you about before. The one that magically appeared from under a table at the Big Pipe booth."

"That's great," Justin laughs, "Sounds like fate has it you guys are to meet again."

"I'm intrigued," I say with a flirtatious smile.

"First things first," Kat replies as she snatches the Magic Beans out of my hand again and starts directing Jen to the bathroom. "Let's see if this faux co is any better than the last shit I tried before, come on Jen." They walk towards the ladies' room, giggling. We all look at each other and grin.

"All right, I guess we should head into the gentlemen's room and see for ourselves," Billy states.

We jump up from our barstools and head to the lavatories, and in each bathroom stall, you hear sniffling.

Sniff..." Ouch, that shit burns!" I hear Billy say.

"Damn, you aren't kidding!" Justin shouts out from his stall.

I am still fumbling with my package and then finally get a good scoop, and BAM!

"Holy shit! Yikes, that hurts," I yell, my voice echoes through the restroom. One more to be sure, and I take another big scoop, shoot my head backward. Man, that burns. Its effects quickly overtake the initial burn in my nostrils. It is fantastic. It is like nothing I have ever felt before. It is the high of coke, mixing with a steady, wonderful tranquility feeling.

With this instant euphoric feeling, I am now unbelievably excited and hoping that when I make it back to the bar Kat will be there. I hustle toward the place we had been sitting. My heart is racing. I quickly make it out of the bathroom and around the corner and attempt to glance at the bar. I couldn't see her yet. I walk even faster and peek around the corner, and then I finally see the two girls sitting at the bar where they left us. They are both laughing as we walk up.

"So how did it go, guys?" Kat says. "You guys feeling groovy?"

"Yeah," I answer." It burns like hell, but I love it…"

Kat says, "yea, that shit burns like a fucker."

I love her accent. "So, where are you from?" I ask. I am feeling exceptional, and everything felt astonishing.

"I grew up in Atlanta," she responds. "How about you guys?"

"We live in Tampa. Well, I'm originally from New York." I say. I always like to throw that in there; I am a proud New Yorker.

"Well, hey there, Kevin from Tampa and New York," she says with an even bigger smile. We are all beaming and grinning from the magic bean fairy dust powder. Wow, I might have a crush on Kat. I cannot get enough of her. Kat tells us she is a partner, with her ex-husband, in Big Pipe, an LSU graduate with a CPA license. Kat also clarifies that she loves to party. Around thirty years old, she is in great shape, or so it appears. I am into her. I think about Karen momentarily, but I am not letting the responsibility hold me back or bring me down in this magical moment, no way.

Billy says, "Why don't you guys come to that party at the Real-

World Suite that those Jack's Magic Beans guys are having?"

"Fuck yeah," Kat yells.

Then her friend Jen says, "Yeah, let's do it!"

"Yes, let's go!" I shout as I rise to my feet. "It's Limo time now, guys. No more cabs!" I state.

"Agreed," says Justin and Billy.

24

Real World Suite

A quick and comfortable limo trip to the Palms Resort; a few more sniffs around, and the magic beans vanish. We embrace the rolls of euphoric radiance as we step out of the limo feeling like famous people. Floating along, it seems we are so high our feet barely touch the ground as we walk together toward the lobby. *Blinded by the Light*, by Bruce Springsteen, is playing inside the entrance; I can hear the lyrics *revved up like a deuce, another runner in the night.* The beans have me feeling like a rock star in Vegas, and nothing is bringing me down. Once inside the resort, we make our way to the real-world suite party.

The Palms Resort is an adventure to behold. The ten thousand square foot resort and casino have been around since 2000. Home to several world-famous restaurants and nightclubs, the resort has some of the most expensive suites and sprawling outdoor swimming pools and bars.

Entering the suite, we look up and around the room in silence for a minute or two with our watery eyes and powdery noses and notice that everyone is so pleasant. Happy. I remember peering over at all my new comrades and feeling so overwhelmingly alive. I know those magic beans have something to do with it, but at this moment, I love this—sizable white powder piles all over different areas of the room. We walk silently straight to one region, and one by one, we do a few lines.

"This place is excellent," says Jen.

"No shit, nice," confirms Justin.

A familiar face walks toward us as we order some cocktails; he looks familiar to me. I remember it is Alex from the trade show.

"Hey guys, I'm Alex. I'm glad you guys could make it. I see you brought some friends." He smiles, and the girls smile back at him and wave.

"Yes, we did," I say. "I hope that's okay," I wonder.

"Yes," says Alex. "As long as your friends are girls, that is always okay."

"Absolutely," I respond.

"Well, absolutely no business talk tonight," Alex states. "Have fun and enjoy yourselves."

As he walks away, I look back over at Kat, and she is staring at me with a big smile, so I grab her hand and pull her away from the crowd.

"Come, take a walk with me," I say, and we make our way toward the balcony away from anyone else. We both lean up against the railing and look out at the Vegas Strip. The lights are dazzling, and so is she, I admire.

"So, y'all are some of those spice guys, I guess?" Kat asks.

"Yep, that's us; a little over a year ago, I was doing mortgages, and now it's the spice or pot-pourri, whatever you want to call it," I laugh and say.

"Hey, I don't blame y'all," she says. "I know a lot of guys are making a lot of money off of that stuff."

Then she leans in toward me and mutters, "I'm thinking many of these guys are making millions doing it. Some of my best customers start in spice, and now they all own smoke shops all over the place. It's great for us, too, because they are purchasing our merchandise."

"I know," I say smoothly. "The best thing that's ever happened to me."

I lean in and whisper, "I'm thinking I'm going to kiss you now."

"Well, hell, ya better do it fast, or I'm going to have to run away." Without hesitation, I go for it; I gently touch the sides of her face and come in close. Our lips touch briefly, and with a quick, delicate taste of ecstasy, I pull away. It has been a long time since anything like this has happened, and I am enjoying it thoroughly.

Alex, in the suit, appears again, and this time he is with a beautiful smiling lady on his arm and says, "You guys want to join us in the VIP room?"

Kat immediately responds," Hell yeah, lead the way, honey."

We follow Alex and his miss through a hidden side door and into a large bedroom. The lights are very dim, music pumping, and another massive pile of magic beans on the table.

Pointing to the table, Alex says, "Special reserve for VIP's only. This shit is the best there is." Kat and I both spin right over to the counter to help ourselves.

I gesture to Kat and say, "After you, my lady." She sniffs a considerable length of the powdery substance. Impressive. It is my turn, so I want to match what she did. I do mine and sit on the bed's edge with Alex's girl; I feel spectacular, my body

141

buzzing. Alex's girl is so gorgeous, unusually beaming; I feel unfamiliar with this party scene.

"Are you new clients of Alex?" The girl asks.

"Not me," says Kat. "I'm just here for the beans." The girls laugh together and seem to be comfortable chatting.

"Maybe I could be a new client," I say, "I like these magic beans, and it looks like you are enjoying them too."

"I just feel so wonderful," the girl replies. "I'm just super lucky right now. I don't know what else to say." Not much needs to be said; I have no words for my body's music and feeling. We chill out, and everything seems surreal.

"So, you are selling a lot of these magic beans?" I question Alex. "It looks like you guys have some cash at your disposal, that's for sure.

"We are a group of attorneys based in California," Alex replies, "We're selling to a few large customers and are observing this industry to see how it's going to progress. At this stage, it's more for curiosity than for profit."

"Interesting," I say. "It seems like all walks of life are getting into this game, interesting times."

"No business talk tonight. Right now, it's about pleasure," Alex exclaims. He extends his hand to the smiling girl and pulls her up off the bed.

"You have my card. It is nice meeting you both. Have a good night, Kevin and Kat." The pretty girl takes Alex's hand, gets up off the bed with his help, and leaves the room. He looks back at us with the last grin as he makes his way into a bedroom. I scoot over on the bed toward Kat, and I give her another quick kiss. I get up and extend my hand for her, and she scoffs.

"Don't you be trying to copy smooth dudes' moves," she says as she gets up on her own and gives me a smirk. "You think you're all that, don't you?"

I smile at her, and we walk out of the room back to the main party space. As we are leaving the VIP room, we both turn around to look at the place. We are in awe and give each other a quick look and laugh out loud.

We make it back over to where our friends were before, and they are all gone.

We find the exit and then take the elevator back down to the lobby and make our way through the casino, designed like a maze. We go to a bar and have one more drink, and people watched. It is probably six am by now, but the place is lively. People are winning, people losing, people hooking up, and hookers working tricks.

When we left the bar and passed a couple arguing near the check-in, we saw what I guess is a rugby team in a restaurant food court area eating like they hadn't eaten in weeks. Just a regular night in Vegas, I suppose. Finally, we are back outside, and we see the cab line.

Kat smiles at me and says, "I got to head back and get some sleep before the show. I've barely slept in two days." The sun is peeking up over the horizon and shining on the strip. I give her one last kiss and open the door of her cab, respectfully.

"See you soon," I say.

With a little sassy attitude, she responds, "Maybe." She winks, grins, and closes the cab door. She rolls the window down.

"Definitely," I say as I wave goodbye. The cab pulls away toward the rising sunlight. I think to myself as I walk toward my cab, what a crazy night.

25

Peculiar Wares

I somehow make my way to the Aria hotel where we are staying. I quietly slip into the room where everyone sleeps and sneak into bed. What seems like five minutes later, I am awoken by Justin screaming.

"Hey, lover boy, time to get up!"

"No way. Please leave me alone. Need sleep," I mumble and pull the blankets over my head.

He hollers back at me, saying, "So did you get some or what? I hope so with all the time you spent with her."

"Nope," I respond. "I'm a gentleman; I would never pressure a lady on a first date."

"So, no? That sucks. We didn't know where you guys went, so we all got out of there and went to Caesar Palace and some nightclubs. Fantastic time. We're going to get something to eat. You want to come?" Justin asks.

"No way, dude. You go. I need to sleep." Another five-minute time warp, and they are back and wake me up again. I realize that is all the sleep I am getting, and so I am up.

Back at the *CHAMPS* trade show again, and it is looking

like more of the same. The music is pumping again from the same spot. I see Kat at her booth a few aisles over, but I am keeping my distance for now. We are meeting a few people about some potentially large deals, and the *Peculiar Wares* guys have a competitive edge.

"So, when are we meeting Lloyd and Jay from *Peculiar*?" I ask Billy.

"I spoke with Stan an hour ago, and he said they would meet us over at the booth around three."

"The *Geno-trition* booth?" Justin asks.

"Yes, the booty shaker-*trition* booth," Billy replies.

We make our rounds through the rows and rows of booths. A lot of the stuff looks the same as everyone else's. There are tons of sexy promo models selling many silly products. I am enjoying the eye candy.

Stan comes walking over to the guys and me and says, "What's up, guys? Good to see you. You guys have a minute to talk? I want to clarify a few things." He pulls out a little notebook and pen. He asks, "So, for the chem's, what kind of quantity do you guys want to purchase from *Geno-trition*?"

Billy responds, "We want to do thirty-five kilos of AM-2201, ten keys of JWH-210, and five keys of 5-Me0-DALT." Stan scribbles it down in his notebook.

"Ok, cool. I'll send an invoice for those. Okay, next up, I want to go over *Peculiar Wares* quickly before Lloyd and Jay get here. I know they have a falling out with their last manufacturer, shipping them an inferior product. A product that did not have the correct cannabinoids or that had any at all. These guys are killing it right now and adding franchises every week."

"Damn," I say. "How many stores do they have?"

"Twenty-three, but more are coming on all the time."

"That's crazy," Billy says. "What makes *Peculiar Wares* so great? What do their stores have that others don't?"

Stan responds, "Their attorney has a letter from the Louisiana Attorney General's office allowing them to sell their *Cobra Kai* product in stores for up to two years. So, any *Peculiar Wares* owner has special protection from law enforcement."

"What?" Justin asks. "How is that possible? A letter from the Attorney General?"

Stan quickly responds, "That is correct, two years from the Attorney General of Louisiana."

I then add, "And they are selling millions and millions of dollars' worth of *Cobra Kai* pot-pourri?"

"Yes, they are," Stan says with a smile.

"That's crazy," Billy says.

"And here they come now," Stan replies. The two of them come walking up, shake our hands one after the other, and introduce themselves.

"This show is nothing but spice," Lloyd says as he looks around the trade show. "What's up, Stan. How have you been?"

"What's up Lloyd, Hey Jay. How's it going?" Stan responds. "Hey guys, this is Billy's two partners, Justin and Kevin."

"Billy, last we met in Louisiana, sounded like you were the mad chemist of the bunch," Lloyd says.

Billy responds, "Ya, things have been going well, and we're always looking for new partners. Stan here tells us you might need a new supplier. If so, I'd love to talk about it and give you our pitch."

"Whoa, straight to the point," Jay responds. "Yeah, man, we are looking right now. We're adding more stores to our network weekly. Two more since we last spoke to Stan, so it's twenty-five stores today and three more on the way."

"That's exceptional, guys," Stan says. "Having that legal representation is a big part of that growth. That's what the PGA can do for you guys, too." He pats Billy's back.

"We're going to get on board," Billy clarifies. "When we get back to Tampa, we are going to complete a few things. Legal representation being at the top of that list."

Just then, a tap on my shoulder, and I turn around.

"Hey there, spice boy," Kat says with a big smile. "I see y'all are right back at it."

She looks great, and I am excited to see her. I turn away from the meeting and focus on her.

"Hey, Kat. What's up? Did you get any sleep last night?"

Kat says, "Yeah, a little. I am surprised I slept at all with how much of that Faux Co we did last night."

"I know right," I say. "That shit is great. So, how's your day going?"

"I hate these fucking shows," she confesses. "These douchebag smoke shop owners are all looking for big discounts." We both laugh and agree.

"Well, I won't haggle with you. Just give me your price list, and we'll put in an order," I say.

Kat responds, "You don't have to, that's ok. I'm not trying to go around hooking up with people to get their business."

We laugh again, and then I say, "Hey, let's go out that side entrance." I pull out a joint and show her. "I need a pick me up; I saw a bunch of heads puffing away out there; let's go."

"Yeah, let's go. Let me grab my drink over at the booth first," Kat says. "And I'll tell Cliff I'm taking a break really quickly."

"So, Cliff is your ex, but you still work with him? How does that work?" I ask.

"It works, I handle the accounting, payroll, and stuff, and he handles the sales. His girlfriend has been helping him out too, but she is annoying as hell. If she doesn't change her attitude, I'm going to have to fire her ass!"

We both walk over to the Big Pipe booth, and she grabs her jack and coke and yells to Cliff, "I'll be back in thirty!"

"Yeah," Cliff replies, and then we head out the exit door and over to a nice corner area, and I fire up the spliff. I take a few puffs and then pass it to her.

She takes another puff and says, "That's all for me. I'm more of a stimulant kind of girl. Pot makes me sleepy. My drug of choice is white."

"Pot is my number one, then drinking and some occasional cha-cha."

Kat laughs, "ChaCha? Is the Faux Co considered cha too?"

"I guess you could say that," I respond. "Especially that shit from last night. Mephedrone is freaking amazing. All those cheerful people in that suite room? That shit was weird."

Kat laughs again and says, "I know right, it was like everyone was on happy juice or something crazy, but I felt amazing."

I put out the joint and throw it in the ashtray and say, "I better get back over to that business meeting that just started before I walked away."

Kat says, "Oh shit, I'm sorry. Did I drag you away from all that?"

"No worries. Billy and Justin can handle it. I'm not worried." I respond.

Kat says, "You're lucky if you have partners you can trust. I've had so many problems with partners and employees."

"And ex's," I say with a chuckle.

"And ex's," she responds. "Count your blessings if you can

trust them… Do you trust them?"

"Totally," I reply. "My partners have given me no reason not to."

"Then you're lucky!" she says. "Are all of you going to the Glow party tonight? Those guys throw perfect parties. Free drinks and free food usually."

"Yeah, I'd love to go with you, Kat," I say with a grin. "Thanks for asking. I'll bring the magic beans again."

Kat looks at me and says, "Well, I'll be there. If you guys end up going, just let me know."

"We're going—no doubt about it. Maybe I should head back over to the guys before they get pissed. Let me see you back to your booth Ms. Kat."

"There you go again, trying to be all smooth. Just buttering me up, player," Kat replies.

In my best British accent, I respond, "I don't have the foggiest idea of what you are referring to, Ms. Kat, but I can assure you there is no foul play at hand. None."

"You're weird!" she says, "Let me get away from you before you blow it."

She likes me, I can tell. Sometimes the stars align, and everything flows so smoothly. This moment is one of those occasions. I determine I will not miss this opportunity, and for some strange reason, I know it.

26

Glow Party

We walk back to the Big Pipe booth, and I say goodbye to Kat for now. I turn to leave and follow the music's sound all the way back to the booty shaker-genomics booth where all the guys are still standing together.

Billy is talking, "So fifty pounds of mix with 5Me0-DALT would take us just a few days to ship. Not a problem at all, guys. Hey Kev, we are just finishing up. I can fill you in later."

"Sorry, guys, I had to speak with someone else about placing an order. Hey, is everyone going to the Glow party tonight? I've heard some good things about it," I say.

"Glow always throws grand parties," Jay relates. "They spend a shit ton of money on them. We're all going."

Justin says, "Yo, you guys have to go over to Jack's magic Beans booth and get some free samples. That shit is outstanding. I still have a few from last night, I think."

"Yeah, their booth is in the back-right corner of the show. It would be best if you grab some," I reply.

"Jack's Magic Beans? Stan asks. "Do you know what

substance is in it? Is it MDPV?"

"It's Mephedrone, and it is solid," Billy says.

"Where is this booth? Let's go over there," Lloyd questions as he chuckles.

"Good meeting you guys. Let's meet up at the Glow party later." We all start shaking hands and saying nice to meet you and goodbye as Justin gives me a tug on my arm.

"Dude, let's take a walk," He says as we walk away.

"Billy, you are coming. Let's go somewhere so we can go over everything that just happened." We make it over to the food area and pull up a few chairs to talk. Justin is as excited as ever.

"Ok, so these guys want us to make them fifty pounds to start with that 5Me0 shit. And then a hundred a week after that. Holy shit, dude."

"5Me0-DALT. What is that, and what's its legal status?" I ask.

Billy responds, "It's a psychedelic of the tryptamine class. It's not illegal, but it falls into that gray area of analogs, not one hundred percent out of watchful eyes. That's why we need that attorney to give us a letter telling us it is ok and then we will be fine."

I respond, "That Jim D. guy. I am on it."

Justin says, "So, there are those guys at *Peculiar Wares*, and then there's Morene Wholesale. While we were standing at the booth, when you left, Hammon came over to us."

"Ah, I missed Hammon? He's a good customer," I say.

"Yeah, well, Hammon wants better pricing. We told him to get his orders up, and we can work with him. He says if we can get him to under two dollars per gram, he will buy a minimum of one hundred fifty thousand a month!"

"Holy Shit!" I cheer. "This all happened when I stepped away for fifteen minutes?"

"Yep," Billy says. "Next time, don't go wandering off with whatever strange Big Pipe girl that comes along."

"With our current customers, Morene picking up his orders and *Peculiar Wares* new orders that put us near one million a month in sales," I say.

"Fuck, yes!" Justin shouts.

"And that's only the beginning," Billy says. "With Stan supplying us with legal help and customers, Johnny and Lou supply us with cheaper chemicals. Both the New York and Florida warehouses ready to ship product, we are on the verge of a lot more."

"Alright, Let's get out of here," Justin says. "Let's go back and relax for a little while, and then we're supposed to go to that Brazilian meat restaurant with Chris, and then we'll go to the Glow party."

"Yeah, let's go. I've had enough of this place," Billy says. I agree, and we go outside and head back to the Aria hotel. After a colossal steakhouse meal with the guys, we rest and dress for a night out for the last time while we are here in Vegas.

Justin, Billy, and I proceed to the Glow Party, where the lights and music elevate. We walk in, and I find a cozy-looking seat by the bar; I get my usual Vegas drink, Jack and coke. I am tasting my beverage, thinking about this wild trip, this unbelievable journey. When Kat silently slips by my observation and sits in the seat next to me. I speak nothing and grin; she smiles back at me; she is pleased to see me, I can tell. She relaxes at the bar and locks her leg around mine; she grabs my arm as we sit and whisper.

"I'm happy to see you again," she whispers and squeezes me a tad.

"Wait a minute," I respond. "You've been playing tough-girl the entire time, and now you're showing me some affection? Is my smoothness finally getting to you, or did you already start on the magic beans?" She squints her eyes at me with an angry look, then cracks a cutesy smile.

I laugh and respond, "Oh, that's it! It's the beans that have got you going. Maybe I should take a trip to the bathroom to catch up. I'm feeling like I'm a little behind you right now. That shit burns, though. But I guess I must…"

"You don't have to go to the bathroom. Just put it in your drink and stir; it works like a charm. I can't snort any more of that shit. My nose freezes up, and I can't breathe at all," Kat states.

I ask, "Really, that works? Just mix it in?"

"Fuck yeah," Kat answers. "And you don't have to bother with those trips to the bathroom either. Just sip and go; it is the only way to enjoy it thoroughly." So, I pull out a pack and drop it in my drink while hiding it under the bar. A quick stir and it dissolves right away. I am ready. I sip my new favorite beverage, Jack's Magic Beans and Coke. It does not take long before I am on a different level. The party is relaxing, and everyone is in a great mood. We are all riding high and loving life.

When the party ends, many of us walk around from place to place—walking and watching. I am holding Kat's arm as we walk, and it almost felt like an out-of-body experience as I glide along with what felt like no effort at all. We end up back at the Aria suites in another chem supplier's suite party, and the drinks and the beans keep spreading.

Like a dream, Justin says, "We must catch a flight in a few hours, dudes. Maybe we should stop and go to bed." No one listens to the voice of reason in these moments. The sun is now up, and I convince Kat to come back to my room. We stumble into bed, but neither one of us even tries to take off our clothes, and we pass out.

Two hours later, my alarm is going off, and I wake up. I immediately feel the stabbing pain between my eyes and temples; I feel like death. Justin and Billy have already packed their suitcases and are almost ready to go.

Billy says, "Dude, you have some dark circles under those eyes." I look in the mirror, and holy shit, I look worse than I feel, which is fucking awful. The rest of that day is like hell on earth. Riding in our limo to the airport is downright horrible.

I am lying on the floor at the terminal, nauseous. Taking off in an airplane is a near-death experience for me. I have never felt a hangover like this before. I honestly thought I might have a heart attack and die on the spot. There comes the point for all party animals when you realize you can't keep doing what you used to do when you were twenty. That feeling will stick with me. Near-death hangover aside, I am on top of the world with my new business, new business partners, and a new girlfriend—time to take this shit to the next level.

27

Taco Night

After nursing, what seems to be a three-day hangover; it is time to get back to work. I schedule a meeting with the attorney Jim D, the only Cannabinoid lawyer in the Tampa area. He has an office ten minutes from my house.

Billy, Justin, and I go to the attorney's office to introduce and discuss Hot Wax. Mr. Jim D. is very calm and somewhat guarded in our conversation. I figure he is sizing us up to see if we are legitimate businessmen or only some guys looking to scam him and the public. He also let us know that we do not have to operate out of New York anymore and can legally conduct business in Florida.

After our brief introduction to the attorney, we immediately start planning our exit from the Empire State. To start, we will get out of the warehouse's leases and the house we rented for the employees. We would still need a few of the guys we had hired from the New York office, and our manager Michael jumps at the chance to move from Long Island to Tampa.

Next on the list is a new, more massive, more isolated warehouse in Tampa to produce our product. Within three weeks, we move into the new warehouse and are beginning ramp up for phase three.

Our new attorney, Mr. Jim D, says he will get us a list of every state with the legality for each substance we are using. I then get a call from him at around three in the afternoon.

"Hey Kevin, it's Jim D. How are you doing?" He is so cordial and calm.

"I'm good. What is up, Jim?" I ask.

"I'm getting that list finished up for you guys, and I hope to meet with you in an informal setting to discuss a few things with you if that were possible."

"Ok, if you want to do it today, I'm making tacos for my kids at around six. You're welcome to join us." I say.

"Taco night with the family? Ok, sounds great. I will see you around six then. Ok. Goodbye."

That seems a little stiff, but I realize that is who he is—a little awkward.

I am home with the kids, putting the ground beef in the frying pan and cooking. The meat is sizzling when I hear a knock at the door. I quickly turn down the heat on the stove. My five-year-old son, Dylan, runs to answer the door with me.

Jim D. walks in. "Hello. Good to see you, Kevin. Hello little guy."

"That's Dylan," I say. "He's my oldest. Jacob and my wife Karen are napping. Jacob is one."

Jim D. hunches, overlooking Dylan, and says, "Hello, Dylan. Nice to meet you. I'm Jim." All of us shake hands, and I respond, "Come on into the kitchen. I am cooking away right now. Can I get you anything? Water or beer?"

"No thanks, I'm good, nice place you have here. I know this neighborhood is taking off right now. How long have you lived here?" Jim asks.

"Around six years now," I say. "There have been a bunch of demolitions on this block. My house used to be the nice one on the block, but not anymore. Come, take a seat?" I point to a chair at the table.

"Here you go," I say as I pull the chair out for him to sit. He hesitates for a moment and then sits down.

"So, what's up?" I ask. "Is everything ok?"

"Yes, yes," he responds. "Maybe I will have water. It's been a busy day."

I grab water for him and ask, "So how's the state-by-state list coming along? Have there been any updates to the list lately?"

"Yes, I'm almost done with it. I want to make sure it is complete before I send it out."

"And a letter from you that states our business is legal?" I ask.

"Yes, for that, I must see your warehouse and review what chemicals you are using. We can set that up for sometime next week if you'd like."

"Yes, I'd like to do that as soon as possible," I say. "Our guy Stan has told us we should get that taken care of right away."

Jim asks, "Stan from the PGA, right?"

"Yes. Stan had suggested we meet with you."

"Yes, I'm familiar with what Stan and the PGA have going on, but I'm not sure if they are going about it in the right manner," Jim says.

"Oh?" I ask, "What are they doing?"

"A unique philosophy, I would say. Not a big deal. So is your wife eating?" Jim inquires.

"She may make an appearance. She is napping with my youngest. So, what's up, Jim? Is there anything going on I

157

should know about?" I wonder what this guy is doing. He seems tense, uncomfortable.

Jim says, "No, nothing going on. Sometimes I like to visit my clients and visit their families and get a bit of a comfort level with them."

"Ok, Jim. I guess I can understand that. And what about you? What made you choose this industry?"

"I saw a need. Some local businessmen were having some issues with local law enforcement, and I felt like they weren't getting a fair shake." Jim responds, "I also think most people are doing what's right, and the industry's fluidity interests me. I do not know if my parents, who are attorneys, would agree, though. They think I'm like a shooting star, burn bright and fade away."

"Well, I'm glad you are here now," I say. "We need all the help we can get. With all these constant changes and banning of substances, it's getting harder and harder to keep up with it all."

"I'm on it," he responds. "Not to worry."

Jim, Dylan, and I eat some tacos and small talk for a bit, and then he leaves. He is sizing me up and seeing if I am a decent person or not. The next morning, he emails over the state-by-state list. Now we need that attorney letter from him, and we will be golden.

28

Infidelity

I am walking up to my house around five-thirty from a long day at work. My feet can hardly lift as I march because I am so drained. I approach my front door just as Karen is walking out.

"See ya," she says as she escapes in her vehicle and peels out of the driveway. I can hear Jacob crying upstairs, and I knew I am in for a fun night.

Dylan runs over to me, arms wide, and gives me a big hug, and says, "Dad!" It makes everything that much more enjoyable. The love I feel for my kids and them for me is beyond comparison with anything. Right away, I wonder, though, she's been going out a lot lately. She never tells me anything about where she's going or with whom she is going—time to look at her phone history on my mobile phone online account.

I log in, and I can view the record; she calls someone several times before I get home and one call in the last two minutes to the same number. I pay the dollar to reverse lookup the phone number, and some guy's name comes up. I put the first and last name on google, and I can see who it is. A thirty-something single guy I have never heard of before. Uh, oh, here we go again.

An hour later, I log in again, and there is a new number she has just called. I google it, and it is Scores Strip Club. What the hell is this shit, I wonder? I guess Karen is meeting this guy at the strip club. Now I am pissed. I subsequently put Jacob and Dylan to bed for the night, and I wait, on the couch, in the dark, for her to get back home.

2:42 am, I hear a car door close, and a second later, the keys jingling at the front door. I hear her footsteps walking toward the kitchen.

"Well, hello there," I say ominously. "Glad you could make it back home."

Startled, she jumps and clutches her chest and says, "Whoa, what are you doing up this late, babe?" she inquires.

"Just waiting to see your lovely face, babe," I sarcastically respond as I rise slowly. I walk toward her to get a better glance at the face of dishonesty.

"I heard you were at Scores tonight. How was that?" I ask confidently.

Karen looks at me as if I have three heads and asks, "What? Who told you that?" She rolls her eyes and putting her bag and keys away, annoyed; she snubs me and pretends I am not in the room. I make up a story about a mutual friend seeing her out to cover my snooping.

"Sean saw you there; he tried to go over to you, but you were with some guys, so he felt awkward."

She strolls past me and goes up the stairs and asks, "Sean? What did he say?"

"He said he saw you at Scores. What were you doing at

Scores, and who is the dude you were with?" I question.

She tries to blow me off, responding, "Sean doesn't know what he is saying. Why don't you have Sean call me, and I'll tell him what I am doing?"

"What the hell, Karen," I shout up the stairs as she turns and walks up.

"I'm tired; I'm going to bed," she scoffs and slams the bedroom door shut.

I run up the stairs, but she locks the door. I just caught her cheating again; I am sure of it. My next thought is I'm calling Kat tomorrow and taking a trip to Atlanta, Georgia, for some sweet, sweet payback.

That's the way the rest of 2011 went for the two of us. Karen and I cheat on each other every chance we can get. It is a pathetic existence, but I do not believe there is any way out of my situation. I have two young boys to worry about now, which makes the offense sink in even more.

In my defense, I do no local cheating. I never want to hook up with anyone in my area because I feel that is too much disrespect. Any affair is wrong, but I do not care now; I am hurting. Still young and stupid, I guess.

At least I have Kat. I fly into Atlanta and spend a night every few weeks. She is an excellent escape for me, but we turn into more drug buddies than fuck buddies when we are together. Some nights we got so fucked up that we do not even do anything sexual. Even though I know Kat and I will never amount to anything long term serious, it still feels good to have fun with someone.

My marriage is an absolute disgrace, this is certain, but as the months roll by, the cash keeps rolling in. The money we are making is just plain stupid. Me, Billy, and Justin all started acting like idiots. Stupid people that make silly money do dumb things.

I suddenly want an RV, so I go on Craigslist and do a search. I find the one I like, go to look at it with cash in hand, and buy it—a twenty-nine-foot Winnebago. The generator does not work, and the engine is making a noise, but I want it so badly I do not care. It is a sweet ride. It has a nice kitchen, a separate bedroom, and a full bathroom. I will drive the family down to Cape Coral and spend the weekend parked next to Karen's mom and stepdad, Drew's house.

One Sunday afternoon, we head back to Tampa, and Drew' mom, Irma, needs a ride with us, so I happily offer to take her. Irma is always so lovely to me, and I appreciate her. She lives in one of those elderly person condo residences. It is raining, so I want to pull the RV up to the front under the covered area to avoid getting Irma wet. As I approach the overhang, I look up to see if I have the proper clearance. It appears close, but I think I will secure it. I push the gas pedal to edge it closer, and I feel something hit and jerk; I slow to a crawl and then stop.

I know I have hit the top, so I put it in reverse, and I hear another noise. I gun it in reverse to free it; the AC unit's top has pushed down under the roof. It slides along the top and then pops up when it cleared the lower roof. It is now up higher than the beginning of the roof. When I gunned it in reverse, the condo place's roof completely ripped the AC unit up and forward and then down into the RV ceiling and the back of the RV. A huge gaping hole is now at the top where the AC unit used to be, and it is raining. Stupid people that make silly money do dumb things.

While not as stupid as my RV error, Billy buys a brand-new Chevy Tahoe and has it customized entirely with fixtures and accessories. He purchases massive tires for it, but the tires are so big that he cannot turn the wheel without them rubbing loudly against the wheel well. Every time he turns the wheel, it makes this heavy rubbing sound. It looks sweet, though, so only a little ridiculous.

Justin does his part by buying a Lexus sports car just because it has air-cooled seats. I think his exact words; It's got air conditioning for my balls. I'll take it! Now I understand none of us are stupid, but I will say that you don't always make the intelligent choice when you can gain almost anything you want when you want it.

29

Side Effects

Before we know it, 2012 is upon us. We finish up closing the New York locations and move entirely to Tampa, Florida. All three partners are glad we do not have to fly to New York once every three weeks. That novelty wore off months ago. Now it is just a chore. Time away from my kids to party just isn't as fun as it once was, and the guilt settles in about it. I miss my kids too much; my wife is another story altogether.

With more and more substances becoming banned in the country, there is a big push for anyone to develop an all-natural ingredient mix to give you that high effect. Nothing new out there looks promising at all; honestly, most of it is mere garbage.

The guys from *Shush* sent us what they call an all-natural hash product blend they have made, and when it arrives, I am the first to try it out. I stuff the brown putty-like substance in a bowl and take four or five big tokes.

"Tastes like ass," I respond. I do not feel any effect as far as I can tell. No one else even touches it once they see my test. A few minutes later, Billy gets a call informing him that his truck is ready with his latest upgrade. He needs a ride, so I offer to drive him in my beautiful new Mercedes CLS 550. We get in, buckle up, and I tear out of the parking lot. Both our phones are ringing off the hook. I pull on to the Crosstown Parkway and head west. Billy is shouting on Patty's phone, our Hot Wax manager, and Sean, our worker, tries to bet me he can unlock my mini-safe while I am gone.

We pass Ybor and hug around the turn towards downtown and the Ice Palace, where the Tampa Bay Lightning plays. Up ahead, I notice a merge because of roadwork. I felt a little shaky. Billy is still screaming at Patty, and I tell Sean I have to get off the phone. I feel sick like I am going to puke. Billy is still screaming, and I feel light-headed. I cannot get off or slow down because there is nowhere to drive except to merge one lane of traffic cones with tight spacing.

Billy yells, "Kevin, look out!"

A few seconds later, I wake up in the driver's seat, and Billy is steering the car.

"Kevin! Are you ok? Dude, what's up? Are you ok?" He is trying to wake me, and he is shaking me.

I am entirely out of it. I try to take the wheel and slam my foot on the gas, but luckily Billy put the car in neutral, thank goodness.

"Kevin, are you ok? We need to get off at this exit coming up over to the right dude. C'mon, dude, you got to wake up and get us off this road. Yes, to the right. Slow, go slow…"

I finally start coming around and can get off at the Willow Ave exit.

"Holy shit! I shout. "I'm sorry, man. I don't know what happened; I'm sorry." I keep telling him I am sorry repeatedly.

We come to a complete stop; I park and get out of the car. I still feel unbelievably nauseous. I am taking deep breaths and shaking my head, trying to piece together what just happened. I passed out in a tight space with cars in front and behind me, and somehow, we came out of it without a scratch. Shout out to Billy for pulling that shit off. What happened? Does this have anything to do with the new all-natural hash product *Shush* sent me?

Billy drives us to my house, and I still feel like I am going to throw up. We walk together inside, and I look in the mirror; I look like a ghost. Super pasty white. Not attractive. I walk out of my bathroom and stop to look at Billy.

"Do you think you should go to the hospital?" Billy asks. "You don't look so good."

"Holy shit, let me lay down for a minute," I nervously say as I make my way to the couch to lie down.

I lay on the couch for a minute or two and then stand back up to test my stability.

"I don't know what the hell just happened, but I might have had a heart attack or something, so I think I have to go. I really don't want to go, but I have to, right?"

"Yeah, man, go. I'll call Justin, and he can get his wife, Dr. Jill, to get you admitted right away."

He drives me right to the front emergency entrance. I slowly make my way inside and up to the counter.

"Hello, I'm not feeling well, and I'd like to see a doctor," I say.

"Yes, sir, you look very pale. Sit down; I'll bring you the paperwork." The lady at the counter says kindly. Still feeling terrible, I fill everything out, and then I see Jill walking over to me.

She smiles and says, "Oh my god, Kevin, what happened?

166

Are you ok? Geez, you look white. You alright?"

"Eh, I've definitely felt better."

"Ok, our staff will be out in a minute, and then we'll take you to your room, and they can run some tests. Just hang in there." She gives me a reassuring pat on my wrist and heads back through the swinging doors. Over the next two hours, they take my blood, give me a CT scan, and wait for the results. Karen, Dylan, and Jacob show up to greet me. It is good to see my boys. Then Dr. Jill comes back in, and another nurse tells me my blood is good, so there are no problems. No heart attack or stroke either. They would get back to me on the scan, but they all look good as far as they tell me. A few minutes later, an older white male doctor comes in and gives me his evaluation.

"Well, Mr. Miller, everything seems to be normal as far as we can tell. Your blood sugar is a tad bit high, but that's no big deal. There is one thing I'd like to point out. Marijuana is in your system; I think it's time for you to stop that. It's time to cut that out, I'd say. Right!" He laughs loudly, but I do not find the joke funny.

I say, "Yeah." Silently, I am thinking, suck my balls, dude! Don't come at me like that. Douchebag! As soon as I go home, I'm going to rip a fatty. So, when I get home, that's what I do, and it feels magnificent. It was quite an eventful day. Sitting out in my house's backyard, on my patio chair, looking up at the stars relaxing as I puff, and my anxiety melts away.

I wonder if my sample of the spice I smoked earlier resulted in me blacking out in the car today. I take another puff and recall the scenes of the day. The doctor said he saw weed in my bloodwork, but I know that it is not only natural pot or cannabis; it is the synthetic herbs; the spice. Even if

167

manufacturers claim it is all-natural, it is not entirely.

Lately, I have been reading and hearing rumors; I take another extended draw on my nicely rolled joint, deep breath, and exhale. I recall hearing about people claiming to have had some adverse effects using spice or pot-pourri. I wonder, could this event of near-death in my vehicle result from the pot-pourri and new product sample I tried? I will stay alert. I will read up on any possible adverse side effects of synthetic cannabinoids. Unfortunately, we have criminalized a harmless plant medicine, cannabis. For thousands of years, we have used marijuana for many medical conditions, including anxiety; synthetic copies may not be that safe.

30

ATF Raid Scare

Karen, Titi, Jeannette, and the boys travel to Cupecoy Beach, St. Maarten. They meet my parents at Rainbow Beach Club, their island beach condo, for a leisurely spring family vacation. In the blink of an eye, we are spinning back off down to the Florida Keys for Billy's bachelor party in Key West.

The mild spring quickly turns to sweltering hot, long days of Summer in Florida. Mid-June is the month you wish you were super-rich, so you could head up north for the summer and live the snowbird life, but not when you have kids—not happening.

It is a typical tropical June morning at the warehouse, and it seems like any other day. Worker Justin arrives first and opens the warehouse as usual, and we all come in slowly afterward. Billy is a few minutes late because he must go to FedEx to pick up another overnight shipped package of ten Kilos of AM-2201 from *Geno-trition*. Vince, Justin, and others are getting the packers set up for another large order we need to finish today.

Worker Justin goes out of the back entrance to smoke a

cigarette, and he gets locked out; the door closes behind him and locks. He bangs on the door, but no one hears him, so he shrugs his shoulders and thinks he'd walk around to the front after, no big deal. Justin lights up his butt and starts smoking; Justin notices two blacked out box-trucks and a black minivan parked next to it. He takes another few puffs, and he sees a black SUV with tinted windows pull up, the side door opens, and everyone gets out and starts talking. They are probably around one hundred yards away; he can reasonably see them standing in black uniforms talking. Another black SUV pulls in and parks.

Quietly under his breath, Justin says, "What the hell is going on over there." He glares his eyes and tries to get a better look. The newest SUV's driver door opens, and a guy steps out and gives him a long three-second scowl.

Under his breath, Justin says, "Scott? What the hell is he doing here?" and then it hits him. Scott, my Mom's ex-boyfriend who works for the ATF, just gave me a long, stern warning stare, and now he's talking to a bunch of guys with tinted windows and box-trucks.

"Holy shit," he whispers to himself. "We're getting raided. Holy shit, holy shit." He slowly starts walking his way around the back of the building. Slowly, calmly stepping and then turns the corner out of view and starts running full speed.

He cuts around the front corner of the building and runs in through the front entrance screaming, "Scott is here! Scott is here! We're getting raided! We're getting raided!"

No one has any idea what he is talking about and looks at each other for a second.

"We're getting raided, guys!" He yells, insistently looking wild-eyed and crazy. Suddenly, it hits everyone, and they all start scrambling for the front exit.

"Let's go. Let's go!" Vince yells.

I jump up and start towards the front exit. I walk out, and I see Billy's truck ripping out of the parking lot. Vince runs across the grass field in front of the warehouse. Billy stops and picks Vince up, and then they vanish. I make it just past the front door, and then I feel like I should go back and grab the chemicals and flush them down the toilet. I find them and grab the only two kilos left and run to the bathroom with a pair of scissors. I slice the bag, dump the contents, and flush the toilet. Three flushes and one kilo disappears. I fumble, cutting the next one, I toss and flush, and the second, gone. I stand up and run for the front door and then run straight to my car. I peel out of the driveway, and just like that, we are all gone.

I call my partner Justin on my cell and say, "Dude, what the hell is going on? Who is Scott? Who is raiding us?"

Over the phone, I hear my partner Justin yell back, "Worker Justin says that his Mom's ex-boyfriend Scott, who works for the ATF, just stepped out of a blacked-out SUV. He says there were box trucks in the back, and he says that the Scott man gave him a long stare before he went over to the other people out in the back. Justin thinks we were about to get raided."

Worker Justin interjects from behind me, saying, "Dude, I'm not thinking we were getting raided, I know we were!" Worker Justin says. "He gave me this long fucking stare when he got off his truck, dude. I'm telling you. We were about to get raided."

"No way. What the fuck?" My partner Justin yells.

"I'm telling you, dude!"

My heart is pounding out of my chest, and I say, "Oh my god. What the hell? So, where is everyone going? I'm going to call Billy, and I'll call you back."

I immediately call Billy and say, "Dude, what is going on? Worker Justin is swearing we were about to get raided and that Scott is out back and…"

Billy cuts me off, "I don't know, man. That is crazy. I'm not sure what to think or say right now."

I can overhear Vince screaming and freaking out in the background, "How fucked up is this, dude, fuck. What the hell is going on…?"

"Vince, shut the hell up," Billy yells, "I'm not sure what is going on but let's meet up somewhere, Kevin. Oh shit, I still have all these chemicals in my car I just picked up from FedEx. I need to get rid of this right now."

I scream back, "Don't just dump them. We don't even know if this is real or not. If you don't want to, I will but don't throw the chemicals out!"

"Alright, well, let's get off the phone," Billy says. " I'll handle that, and then we can meet up at Hot Wax in thirty minutes."

We all go to Ybor and meet up in the back of the store. Everyone is in a frenzy. Vince keeps saying, "How fucked up is this? What is going on? Kelly is going to kill me."

"Shut up, Vinny, you're killing me," Billy shouts.

"Yeah, dude, you need to relax," I say. "So, what the hell are we going to do? If that is a raid, why would they let us leave and not chase after us?"

Partner Justin shouts, "Justin, are you sure, man? Who is this guy you saw? Please explain."

"I was out in the back. All these box trucks and SUVs with tinted windows were there, and then a car pulled up, and then, fuckin Scott, my Mom's old boyfriend who works for the ATF, got out and looked at me with this look, dude. He stared at me for a long time and then walked over to the other guys. I know he is trying to tell me something. I am one hundred percent sure of it," worker Justin explains.

Billy responds, "OK, so we need to see my criminal attorney Alex right now if that is true. He's a good friend. We shouldn't even be here. If they're coming for us, we don't want them to come here and maybe confiscate all of our inventory here."

"Could that happen?" I ask.

"I don't know, man, but we need to get to Alex's right now! We shouldn't stay here!" Billy says.

Partner Justin walks to the front, "Let's go." We all head back to our cars.

"I'll text everyone the address. I'm going to call now," Billy says.

I get the address shortly after and start driving that way. It is less than ten minutes away. When I pull in, Billy and Vince are already out of the truck.

Billy says, "Alex is to be back in fifteen minutes from the court, so he says to just head up there, and his partner will let us in his office."

When everyone else arrives, we all head up to this old Victorian home-office floor, at the top of the stairs, greeted by a guy that looks like Jabba the Hutt with a shirt and tie.

"How's it going, fellas? I hear you guys might be in a bit of a pinch? Name's Mark," He says as he shakes everyone's hands. "Come here this way, boys." He walks down a long hallway.

"Right in here. Alex will be back soon. I'll see if Kathy can come in and get you guys something to drink." We all thank him and take a seat in Alex's office. We are all scared, shitless.

Vince starts again with his panic talk, "Kelly is going to kill me. Oh my god, I do not want to hear it from her."

Partner Justin yells out, "Dude, relax. We do not understand

173

what's going on."

"Yeah, dude, you're going to have to calm down," Billy says. "Let's just wait for Alex and see what he has to say." And so we wait.

31

Behind Door Number Two

A few minutes later, Alex comes into the office in his suit and tie.

"What's up, guys? Billy, how's it going?" he goes around the room, introducing himself, and then sits at his desk.

"Alright, Billy, tell me what's going on?"

Billy fills him in with all the details, and then Alex thinks in silence for a few seconds. He is scribbling on a piece of paper, and the sound penetrates the silence and heaviness of the room.

Alex stops writing and looks up, pauses, and says, "Well, the first thing you have to do is check your bank accounts and confirm non-seizure of funds. Have you checked that?" He asks matter-of-factly.

"Holy shit," I say. "I'll look right now. I pull out my phone and log into our Sun Trust bank account.

"Oh, my god. If they take our funds, we are so screwed. Logging in, password, what city am I born in, oh my god, loading… Our funds are still there!"

"Thank god," Justin says with relief.

"Well, you're lucky. The Middle District of Florida is notorious for seizing funds and making you fight to get them back," Alex says.

"But we don't even know if we were even going to get raided," Justin replies. "How can we find out? Are they going to show up at my house tonight?"

"They might," Alex answers. "There is no way to know until they come. It would be best if you guys got to work on getting those funds out of your accounts. I can draw up a retainer agreement, and you can deposit maybe one hundred thousand in my escrow account. Then they can't touch it."

"I have a criminal attorney friend that I can call. Maybe we can transfer a few hundred more to him; I'll find out," I say.

"You should also think about your other assets," Alex mentions. "Billy, didn't you guys buy a condo on the water?"

"Yeah, but what do we do about that?" Billy asks. "The title for it is in the company name. What can we do about all that?"

"The guy you just met, Mark, is a master of asset administration," Alex says. " I'm not even going to explain what he does, but you guys should sit down with him right away and see what your options might be. Just a thought. I think it would be a good idea if you believe that the heat is on."

"This is insane," Vince whimpers. "I feel like I'm going to puke."

Billy looks around at us, he throws his head up and back, and says, "This is confusing; I think I'm going to head home and think about things. If I don't have the cops waiting at my house when I get home, I'll probably do five huge dabs and then drink Ketel One and sodas until I pass out."

Everyone laughs a little; we all look around at each other

and agree it is time to go home.

"Alright, guys, it looks like we all have some work to do," Alex says. "So, who handles the money?"

I raise my hand and say, "That's me."

"OK, so do you have a check, or can you do a wire today?" Alex asks.

"Yeah, I can do that. I can call it in if you give me your wiring instructions." I respond. Everyone gets up to leave.

"Later, guys. I'll be in touch tomorrow," Billy says in a disappointed tone.

Justin yells out as he walks through the door, declaring, "Yeah, hopefully, I don't have five cop cars parked in my driveway when I get home."

"Oh shit, oh no. my car is still at the warehouse!" Vince shouts.

"No way," I say. "Holy shit, Vinny."

Vince shouts and pleads, "Dude, drive me back to get my car. I have to get my car."

"Are you fucking kidding me? I say. "I have to drive you back there now?"

Vince replies, "What am I supposed to tell Kelly when I show up with no car? Take me back."

I cannot believe what is unfolding and reluctantly agree.

"I have to go back to get Vinny's car. Wish us luck." We leave Alex's office, walk toward my Mercedes, jump back in, and begin the trip to ground zero. I am silent the entire ten minutes we take to get to the 78th street exit.

As we turn into the warehouse development, I say, "Holy shit, my heart is pounding, dude." I am crippling with fear now, and I have haunting visions of cops, guns, and prison. I imagine they will wait for us to return, ready to pounce.

"I can't even talk, dude," Vince reacts.

There is a long, straight, and narrow road with speed bumps every twenty yards in the development front. We hit the first bump, and we see an SUV turn the corner and start heading straight towards us along the same narrow street.

"Here comes a freaking blacked-out SUV," Vince softly says as he looks rigid, straight ahead.

"Yeah, I can see it. Here it comes." I whisper and slowly duck down low. We both try to look straight ahead while our eyes are panning hard left. Another speed bump lifts the car, and the SUV is around ten yards away. I can see a person with sunglasses and what appears to be barriers or an enclosure in the vehicle's back. Then he bobbles up his window as we pass; he too continues looking straight ahead.

Vince, with a shaky voice, says, "Did you see that? He rolled up his window when we drove past."

"Yeah, that guy did not look over at us and then rolled up his window."

"What the fuck, dude?" Vince whispers.

We both swing our heads around and look back at the truck as it continues going down the street into the darkness.

"Now, let's see what's behind door number two," I whisper back. We must see who is behind the building where all those trucks were supposedly camping out and ready to pounce on us.

"And there's no one here," Vince shouts. "So maybe that is all a bunch of bullshit this morning, and worker Justin was just super high or something this morning, a paranoid freakazoid!"

There is no one here. Not a single car. Except for Vince's car.

"Maybe we weren't getting raided. I don't know, man," he

says as he steps out of my car.

"So, is there work tomorrow? Should I even come in?" Vince investigates.

"I honestly don't know Vinny. I think we all need to give it a night, and I'll call you in the morning."

I belt out my best Vinny sheep noise jokingly as I pull away, "Mee awww Baaaaaa."

"No sheep sounds, man! That shit is over until further notice!" Vinny says.

I drive out and leave the development and begin my drive home. I am not feeling terrific. I feel excited when I imagine being greeted by my boys at home, but I have an eerie feeling of guilt hanging over me. Would the cops be at my house when I get home?

When I got home, I also know that I will get oodles of love from the boys but zero from Karen. Oh well, I ponder. I have other things I ought to worry about now besides her nonsense. When I arrive, there are no cops at my house to greet me. None of the rest of the partners have any police at their homes, either. None of us know what to do or think about all that just happened. Shit is getting very real.

32

Arrested

Billy and Kelly's wedding is an enjoyable engagement for all of us to attend. The entire crew is here except for Vince. He had a prior arrangement of his own to take part. For the first time in a long time, Karen and I are civil and friendly. We check in our plush hotel room after dinner with everyone. Karen and I go back to the room. We get inside and pour another glass of wine.

I look at her in the eyes and admit, "This is pretty much as good as it gets. We have two healthy kids, we're still young, we're making tons of money, and there are no worries." She looks back, smiles, and agrees. For the first time in a long time, I felt content. Well, maybe a little uneasiness would creep in occasionally. Were we getting raided that day, or is it all just a paranoid-made story in our heads? There is no way to know, and it drives us all a little mad.

The next day at the old Tampa Firefighters Museum in downtown Tampa, my partner Billy marries Kelly, his life's love. The partners all needed a break like this; we were feeling so anxious.

After a few more weeks, the three partners had time to think about everything, and we were all in agreement that it is time to get out. We made millions of dollars, and Hot Wax is on the rise with the new glass blowing window we installed. All the customers walking by on 7th Ave can see live glass blowing right in the window in front of them. We offer Vinny the website to keep on doing some online orders and pay us twenty percent of the gross each week. All the worrying about the phantom raid and what might keep up with the DEA; it got to us. We were all done with living this way.

Now that I am in my semi-retired mode, I am going for a jog. Deep down, we all want to feel like we are part of something, and we have Hot Wax to concentrate on building a community of like-minded people, making our tribe. I figure it is what I have wanted since *the Oak Beach Inn*, the friends and co-workers doing cool shit and enjoying smoking some pot, living our best life—feeling seen and heard and part of a group. So, what if you think I am a pothead? That is me, I suppose, but not in the negative shame way of the past eras. There is a movement of freedom from pot prohibition and societal stigmas. Underground is mainstream, and cannabis is big business. Legalization is on the horizon. Getting medical and recreational cannabis is becoming the standard and norm as alcohol and cigarettes were the eighties' norms. We figured out how to tie it all together in a business and make it cool and inviting, comfortable, relaxing as my living room in my home.

THUMP! THUMP! THUMP!

I am time-warped instantly into this life-altering moment, standing in front of my door naked. Like the television show *Cops*, I am here, and this is happening. Holy shit. I open the door, naked, and they seize me quickly and put my hands

181

behind my back firmly and rest me on the couch.

"Where's the keys?" One of them calls.

"What keys?" I question.

"Never mind. I found the keys!" He takes them off my wood chest near the front door and walks out with a smirk.

"Kevin Miller, you are under arrest. We will take you to the DEA office on Kennedy Boulevard, and Officer Mooney will handle it from there." I do not know if I can fully process his words as he says them; it seems surreal.

"Can I put some clothes on?" I ask.

"We can have someone get your clothes, and you can put them on. Where is your bedroom?" the agent smugly asks.

I am totally out of it, in utter confusion and disbelief. I can barely answer the guy, "Uh, it's upstairs and to the right."

"OK, go get him some clothes and shoes." He points to one of the other guys to go now to my bedroom to get my clothes. He skips up my stairs as if he lives here and shoves my closet door open, and I hear him upstairs boring and pushing in my closet. He comes back down and throws the clothes in my lap, and helps himself to my fridge.

The other officer read me my rights, and with cuffed hands, I awkwardly put on my clothes. They walk me out the front door and towards a police car in the street. I look all around at my neighborhood to see if anyone sees me, and luckily there is no one about, or so you never know, I guess. They shove me in the back of the police car and drive me to jail.

33

Conspiracy to Distribute

J ustin is checking emails and drinking his morning coffee at the office at the same time I am transporting to jail. He hears a knock at the front glass door of the warehouse. He gets up and opens the door, and they grab him and cuff him in seconds. They sit him in a chair when three or four guys run past him to search the building's back.

One agent yells, "I got it. Over here, guys. I think I found them."

He is holding one of our empty Chapstick plastic tubes with Chinese writing on the side. We worked on the containers for another project that diffuses the smell of weed when you blow through it but is still in its early development phase. The agents believe it is synthetic cannabinoids from China.

"Yeah, you found the Chapstick containers. Great job, buddy. You got us now!" Justin states sarcastically.

One agent sees his key-chain hanging on the wall, yanks the Lexus key off it, and walks out the front. Justin's beautiful new Lexus seized. Simultaneously Billy is driving in his new wife Kelly's car when they pull him over and take him in. He is not in his supped-up truck, so it is safe.

Taken to a nondescript building, I must have passed a thousand times but never even noticed before. I get out of the car; I spot Justin escorting in handcuffs behind me. We glance at each other, and neither of us shows any emotion or says a sound. Justin, I, and four agents hold all our computers in boxes on the elevator ride upstairs. Once we arrive in the office, they separate us, and I can see Billy in handcuffs down the hall in another room, just as the officer closes his door.

"Have a seat here," one guy suggests. "Officer Mooney is on his way. He wants to ask you some questions." There's that Mooney name again. Who the hell is Mooney? I question silently. Three officers sit in the painfully silent room together with me. I stare at the floor and start considering what had just happened. I'm under arrest, but I do not understand precisely why. No one is talking to me. The agents are interrogating my partners in the other rooms.

Finally, an hour later, Officer Mooney comes in and sits across from me and says, "Mr. Miller, do you know why you are here?"

Then I realize this is the guy driving the SUV over those speed bumps coming out of our office development that day.

I act simple-minded, "Uh, no, I don't have any idea, but can you tell me, please?"

"You are under arrest for conspiracy to distribute a controlled substance or controlled substance analog. Have we read you your rights?" Officer Mooney asks.

"Yes."

"OK, then I'd like to ask you some questions if that's alright with you?" he asks kindly.

"Yeah, that's fine," I reply.

"So, you are the President of BMS Distributors, correct?" "
Yes."

"And BMS sells products known as pot-pourri or spice?"

"Pot-pourri, yes," I answer.

"So, when did you first realize that you were doing something illegal?"

"Never," I answer. "We did nothing illegal. Everything we did with our attorney's approval, and we had no intention of breaking the law."

"So, what happened between the three partners and Vince?" he asks.

"What are you asking? What happened with Vince? I am confused, sir, please clarify," I respond.

"During our surveillance, we saw Vince peel out in a hurry and scream something to you guys the other day," Officer Mooney says.

I honestly did not know what he is talking about, and I wonder where the hell he is going with it; he continues.

"We've been watching you for months, buddy! Around a month ago at your warehouse, you guys ran out of there like a bunch of scared rats. What was that all about?" Agent Mooney asks.

I have had enough now and say, "OK, now I do not want to talk anymore. I want an attorney."

Mooney responds, "Alright, that's fine. Have it your way. Guys, you can take all these guys to the Marshalls office for processing. Enjoy your day." He stands up, grabs his heavy keys, unlocks the door, and it slams behind him.

We are all escorted in cuffs driven together in a large SUV to the downtown US Marshal's office. The van guys are acting as if nothing happened like we are a passenger in a taxi. Everyone is joking around. It is unusual. We casually discuss how legitimate we are as a business and how we even pay our taxes down to the cent because we know we are under tight scrutiny. We are DNA swabbed and then put in a holding cell. One officer asks me if I have done any drugs recently, and I say not at all. I didn't realize I was going to be piss tested twenty minutes later. Oh well, whoops.

An hour later, we are in front of a judge, and his honor hears the information on the case and does not seem impressed. He makes us sign signature bonds where we put up our house as collateral and go home. Another hour and Karen came to pick me up. It almost seems as if she is happy about my arrest, making it even more annoying—one of those not-so-good kinds of days.

34

Pretrial Release Conditions

The next day, we all have a scheduled meeting with our new Pretrial services officer, Mr. Nathan. Not only do we have to come in the following day to sign up for monitoring, but our wives must go with us. We all must fill out a bunch of forms to sign over our houses as collateral. My lovely wife does not wish to comply.

"I don't have to sign this form!" She snaps. "This isn't my problem; this is your fucking problem. I'm not signing over my house for you."

"I don't have a choice, Karen. Either we sign over the house, or I sit in jail until the trial," I shout.

"So, sit in jail then!" She replies smugly.

Justin's wife, Dr. Jill, hears us arguing and comes over and says, "Karen, come take a walk, let's talk," and she led Karen away into the hallway.

A few minutes later, they walk back in, and Jill says, "Ok, we got it all figured out. We're good. You are alright, Karen?"

Karen nods yes and put her head down. Thank goodness Jill steps in, and Karen finally concedes. We sign the forms, and then we must take another urinalysis. Not only are we in legal difficulty, but they are monitoring, piss testing, and geographically restricting us to the central district of Florida.

Nathan began telling us all how they are restricting our everyday life. I have never gone through anything like this before; I feel the severe weight and gravity. My stomach is tightening with every word of Nathan's communication.

"You must call in every Monday through Friday to check if you will need to report for a urinalysis. If you miss a urinalysis, it is equal to an actual positive test. You will turn yourself in, or we will issue a warrant for your arrest. If you own a firearm, you must surrender it to me immediately. I will conduct home visits once every forty-five days to verify you live at your designated residence. You may not leave Florida's middle district unless you get approval from me, and it better be a good reason, or I will not approve it. Do you understand these terms?"

We all shake our heads and say, "Yes, Sir." We all get up and walk out in total shock and disbelief with that information. Heads are hanging low. We start our way back down the elevator and out to our cars, never even speaking to one another. This will be our new reality, and it sucked.

The girls all leave us and go back to work as the three of us head over to Alex, the attorney, and Jabba the Hutt's office. We have a meeting arranged, and all sit down in his office and start planning. Alex begins with his thoughts.

"So, what we know right now is that they have charged you guys in the Southern Districts of New York intending to distribute a controlled substance or analog. I'm guessing they will try to come after you for violating the Federal Analogue Act. I know they are trying to claim the substances you were using are like a controlled substance. It also mentions if we intended it for human consumption. They also charge your friend Vincent. Any of you have spoken with him? How is that going to play out? I can tell you he is probably going to flip on you guys. Also, I am not licensed in New York. Do any of you guys have an attorney or know any attorneys in New York? You are going to have to get working on that as soon as possible."

I pipe up and say, "I have an old college friend that practices criminal law, I can call him. What about our assets?"

"So, did they seize anything?" Alex asks.

"They took my Mercedes," I shout.

"And my Lexus," Justin shouts back.

"So, they didn't take your car, Billy?" Alex asks.

"No, I was driving Kelly's car when they pulled me over," Billy responds.

Alex laughs and replies, "Lucky bastard." Justin and I are not laughing.

"You guys need to get your assets into an attorney escrow account right away. Once again, you guys each must hire your own attorneys. You can't have one attorney represent you entirely. Hence, all of you guys must start figuring it out. You're lucky. The judge didn't order the release conditions to include a no-contact order, stating that co-defendants cannot communicate with each other pre-trial."

"Our consultant Stan is coming into town tomorrow to go over everything in more detail, but yesterday, the cops arrested ninety people. They seize over thirty-six million dollars. *Operation Log Jam* is the DEA's name for it. I've already reached out to a few attorneys and have narrowed it down to a few. I think we should probably pay a flat fee for at least one attorney representing us. This way, we have one working full time on the case for as long as needed." Billy says.

"That's probably a good idea," Alex says. "Damn guys, I hope you have some cash hidden away somewhere. Either way, start finding out about attorneys for all of you. I won't represent any of you because it's in New York, but I can work with you guys and use my offices for as long as needed."

We stay in the office for around another hour. We keep rehashing the same crap. We tell our stories about what had happened the day before—my car. My beautiful freaking vehicle, gone. Driven away by some smug cop douchebag. Oh yeah, now I don't have a car. My stomach is churning again. What am I going to do about this? How much is it going to cost? Am I going to jail? Time away from my kids sounds terrible. How long could I be in incarceration, potentially? A lot to take in. With that scare a month earlier, I am still shell-shocked and traumatized because we were all just arrested. Now I must call Vince and see how he's doing. Vinny and I are playing phone tag, and I finally reach him around dinner time. I can tell right away from his voice that he is not pleased. As expected, Vince is beside himself emotionally, as are all of us. He persists, asking me if I am going to pay for his lawyer.

"You promised you would take care of me," he repeats. I didn't have much to tell him because our attorneys instructed us not to speak to him. I wanted to say to him all that I knew, but I am too scared. I tell him to hold on and wait to see what would happen, and I would see what I could do for him. I guess I am not very convincing because Vince and his dad hire his own lawyer a few days later, and then it is official. He isn't my friend any longer. He is now my adversary.

Here I am again. Someone was on top of the world and riding

an unbelievable high, now driven into despair. I remember back to my last day up at College after graduation. That same feeling of being on the peak one day, and it's all gone the next. The money isn't coming in anymore. They have my passport, and I am now restricted to Florida's middle district. Worst of all, I cannot even go to my special place at home, in my backyard looking up at the stars and chill with my old friend Mary Jane. Just when I need her the most. How the hell am I going to deal with this, sober? No pot at all for who knows how long. This is my new and unfortunate reality.

35

Operation Log Jam

All these additional problems I am having, and now no cash coming in, either. And when there is no money coming in, I know my pleasant wife will be a difficulty. I can sense that Karen is not putting up with this arrest and lifestyle modification, and she will not go back to feeling deficient and broke. Our already faulty relationship is now at a rupture point.

I call up my old college roommate from Oneonta and non-brother Alex, who moved down to Clearwater nearby. Alex has just gone through a divorce of his own, so I want to get his thoughts on the divorce process. I call him up to say hello.

"Karen and I are not going well at all," I describe to him. "Ever since I got busted, she has been bitter because money is not coming in anymore, and she might have to go back to work. We hate each other."

Alex responds, "If you guys aren't getting along and things are getting worse, your number one goal is to get her ass back to work. If she has a job and is making money on the books, she won't come after you nearly as much. It's all based on your and her income."

"I would never want to be without my kids, though." I reply, "Deep down, I feel like we doom the marriage, but I don't want to hurt my kids."

"The kids are a tough one." he says, " It's the hardest thing about the whole freaking ugly thing called divorce. Just get her working! If nothing else, try for that. Just my take on it."

Having assets but no cash coming in and an unknown attorney expense looming over me. Karen finally lands a job managing paralegal's work for a personal injury lawyer. She is working for a guy named Dick. It seems like a decent job with a respectable guy who graduated from Harvard Law School. Billboards, buses, bus stops, radio, and TV ads, and on and on. The man's face is everywhere.

We hire a nanny, and Karen goes to work. I go to my new full-time job, hanging out at Alex, the Attorney's office, and going over the case. I buy back one of our company's extra Toyota Sequoia from auction for my personal use. Stan comes back into town to act as a legal advisor type and keeps us updated on what is going on with the PGA guys and their legal case.

Stan keeps saying, "There's no way you guys are going to jail. These analog cases are impossible to win, and the government knows it."

"So, what about Jay and Lloyd or Johnny and Lou?" I ask, "Were they arrested?"

"No, none of them. I think that's because of the close relationship that our attorney Don has with the Louisiana Attorney General, Buddy Caldwell," Stan says.

"That's insane," Justin states. "Those guys were doing the same stuff that we were doing, only on a larger scale. And they were selling a hundred million a month or more in chemicals.

Good for them. Sucks for us."

"That is crazy," Billy says.

"No matter what happens with all those guys, I am still here for you." Stan says, "I'll help you any way that I can. I read the complaint, and there's not much basis for it. It talks about Schedule I controlled substance analogs and Billy's contact with Homeland Security. It also drags Vincent into the complaint, which makes little sense."

"Yeah, why is Vince dragged into this?" I ask, "That sucks for him. He was only with us for a few months. He was not with us in New York, and obviously, he's not a partner."

Stan says, "This whole Operation Log Jam is a scare tactic to crush the industry and everyone in it with no actual evidence of intent to break the law. Then down the road, they will say, oh well, our bad. You guys can go now. Oh, and sorry about all those defense attorney fees, and we will keep the seizures. Have a nice day."

All of us shake our heads in silence. Once again, we tell our stories, a little more abbreviated version of this time, and we all go home to sulk. After a few weeks, we all hire attorneys licensed in New York, and those attorneys all believe that the case against us is weak. The attorneys talk about the low percentage of successful defenses in Federal instances and keep using the same stats and legal quotes. You could indict a ham sandwich if you wanted. They keep saying who we are up against and how it is a big deal. The Southern District of New York is known as the most aggressive, well-funded, and prestigious court system globally. If you are misfortunate enough to go up against them, you are in for a fierce, long battle. These are the people that take on Wall Street powerhouses.

Our biggest resolute is the attorney letter from Jim D. It

is the one thing we all feel might be our saving grace. If an attorney tells us that our business is legal, how can there be any intent to break the law? I would argue this question in my head and try to convince myself every night before closing my eyes and attempting to sleep.

36

Deferred Prosecution

In September, we hear a rumor through our group of attorneys that Stan and the guys from *Peculiar Wares* and *Geno-trition*. The cops arrested them. We hear that their attorney Don is also, which shocks everyone. For this to happen to an attorney is a big deal. He must have done something illegal is the equal consensus.

The three of us fly back and forth from New York to meet with our attorneys, and we must appear in court two more times. Every time we must go back to that courthouse, it takes a little living away from us. We are traveling up, meeting with our depressing attorneys, going through the security. You give them your phone, and you take a token. Then up the elevators and to the courtroom. You tremble for your liberty in those places. It's a horrifying feeling.

The Assistant United States attorney that we are going against does not care enough to respond to our attorney's requests or bother to show up in court. When he does, he never even looks at any of us. It is like we are monsters without rights or beliefs. The entire process engulfed us, and it pisses us off to the point of bitterness.

They indict us right before Halloween, and we all wonder if we are going to prison. Still, none of our attorneys can get through to the Assistant United States Attorney, so no one knows what is going on.

Then we hear that Billy's lawyer Tim finally receives a call back from the Assistant United States Attorney. I am waiting for Billy to call me back with the results. He finally calls me back around ten p.m. The cell rings, and I pick it up.

"So, I just got off the phone with Tim, and from what he says, AUSA, Adam might offer us a deferred prosecution in our case," says Billy.

"Deferred prosecution?" I ask. "Prosecution deferred? Until when?"

"The way Tim explains it to me, we will receive amnesty for meeting certain requirements," Billy responds.

"Requirements like what? Probation? Fines? Community service?" I request.

"Yes," Billy replies. "Maybe one, maybe all of those. Not sure yet."

"But either way, we would be off the hook with no legal record, case dropped?" I ask.

"Yes, as long as we don't commit any other crimes or shit like that."

"That's fucking awesome," I say. Holy shit. Is this real? Did we get a break? I am feeling a rush of slight relief. Freedom, we can figure shit out from here—no more bullshit.

"It could be good. Alright, well, let me call Justin. I'm sure he wants to know as soon as possible," Billy says.

"Yeah, yeah, go ahead. I'll talk to you tomorrow." I say. I hang up and cry out, "Yes! Yes!" I run up the stairs to announce to Karen.

"Yeah, babe, it looks like they are dropping the case against us! Yeah, baby!" and I dance around like a clown. I look over at her; all I see is a cold-icy stare.

I stop dancing and say, "You're not happy?"

She replies, "I was hoping you were going to jail, babe."

I yell back at her, "Well, suck my balls, biyatch!"

I am so excited about the news that I will not let her bring me down, so I run back downstairs and pick up Dylan and hug him. Then I grab Jacob and spin him around. I dance with my boys in the living room for a few minutes, showing off my most excellent dad party moves. A little later, she comes down the stairs and still has the same stone face on as she strolls past me.

"Good for you, babe! Good for you," she murmurs.

"Damn, you suck," I say and shake my head. What is her problem, I may never know, but I sure love my boys; she can never take that away from me.

Over the next few days, more information comes in about our deferred prosecution. Our attorneys will have to write up a letter and detail how we are such good people and that we have an attorney letter saying what we were doing is legal. There is never any intent to break the law, and we have kids that rely on us and so forth. We still didn't know about the possibility of fines and probation. We continue drug testing, but it looks promising that we will be clear of all charges.

How long is all this going to take? I need it resolved to move on with my life and get back to my sweet, sweet ganja. Every day without Mary Jane is a little torture of its own.

37

Divorce

Karen must work weekends to make ends meet and have a little extra cash for herself. I do not care too much because I can spend some quality time with Dylan and Jacob. At least she is bringing in something extra to help with everything. Things seem better between us lately; it looks, or maybe that is because I am not seeing her nearly as much as before. Less fighting because of less interaction.

Karen goes out after work occasionally or on a Friday or Saturday night. New friends from work, she tells. No big deal and a bit of a payback for my going out and going on trips over the last few years. My guilt tells me I should let her have a little leeway.

As her going out starts increasing ever so gradually, I get suspicious. She is doing so many things, but I never hear her explain where she is going or who she is going with. On a Saturday night, she said she was going with her niece Yanissa to see the movie Lincoln. I immediately think to myself, Lincoln? Karen is going to a two-and-a-half-hour film about a former president? The girl who can't watch anything for over twenty minutes without her attention span getting the best of her. I don't think so.

She gets home around one am after her "movie." She says nothing and goes into the bathroom for a shower, and then sneaks quietly into bed. My plan is to wait until she falls asleep, and then I will try to find her phone and peek. I do not have to wait for over five minutes, and I can hear her snore.

Slowly getting up, I head down the hall and downstairs. I can see her phone on the kitchen table next to her pocketbook. There is no code on her phone, and I can see all the previous calls. Dick called at 4:34 pm, again at 5:19 pm, and then once more before she left at 5:56 pm. Why would Dick be calling Karen at those times? She is fucking her boss.

Just what I need. I am up for conspiracy to distribute a controlled substance in the Southern Districts of New York, and now this? The world has a funny way of bringing you to the top and slamming you down to the ground. I confront her about it, and she denies it. I tell her to quit her job, and she refuses.

She keeps on saying, "You're crazy. You're ridiculous, and you're pathetic for even thinking such a thing."

Then she tries to turn it on me. She says that if I do not stop acting crazy and paranoid that she will divorce me. Would she divorce me? Something in her head snaps, and she no longer gives a shit; she does not care. Maybe she hates me so much she wants nothing to do with me anymore. Perhaps she saw a golden goose with this prominent ambulance chaser attorney and thinks he will rescue her? It is probably a bit of both. I am in a shitty spot with no alternative escape.

The New Year comes and goes and with it, so does Karen. I am still in legal limbo for an undetermined amount of time, and she is coming and going at will.

I am done with that ridiculous existence and confront her, "I want a divorce. I'm ending your bullshit!" I yell.

"Whatever mother fucker." She responds, "You do what you have to do."

"What the hell is wrong with you? What did I ever do to you?" I shout.

"You know what you did," She yells, "You fucked our nanny, Shannon!"

"WHAT?" I scream. Holy Shit, I would never do something like that, and I had not done that. I never even flirted with the nanny. It is crazy. I know we have both been unfaithful in the past, but having sex with the nanny is something that I would never do. But now I am being accused of it.

"So that's why you're spending so much time with your new boyfriend?" I snap back.

She laughs and says, "Boyfriend? What, you mean, Dick?" she squints her eyes toward me with fierce anger and bitterness.

"Uh, Yeah! Like I don't know?" I sarcastically reply, "Once again, you are confusing me with a stupid person."

She calmly strolls her way out of the house and says, "Whatever do what you have to do." With that, she never returns.

One week later, I have a new lawyer, and another two weeks more, I have filed for divorce. Now I have the distinct honor of being under federal indictment and going through a divorce concurrently.

38

Zen Soma

The months that follow, brutal. Trying to coexist with someone you can't stand and going in for piss tests all the time. Not going to a fraternity brother's reunion music festival trip is brutal.

A friend keeps telling me, "You need to go back out in the field and have some fun. Join Match.com. You'll get ladies constantly!"

I immediately think it sounds interesting. I create my Match profile in a day and start my search. I must admit that it works, and it works quickly. My calendar fills up fast, and I am dating girls while still living with my ex-wife. It is going to take some finagling to make this achievement. I must go to the girl's house or our condo on Treasure Island. The house is a no go.

I date a few girls, and I get contacted by a person nicknamed *Zen Soma* on Match.com. Her actual name, Kimberly. She tells me that Match.com's profile matcher keeps popping me up on her screen, so she figures she would reach out to me. She is fit and trim, beautiful. We go out on a few dates, and it is slowly progressing. I am lucky to meet her. I am not ready to settle down, but I do like Kimberly, so I still dated a few others, and before I know it, she has caught on and then dumps me.

After a few weeks, I send her a text invite asking her to go to *The Ritz*, a concert hall across the street from Hot Wax in Ybor. Luckily, she replies and agrees to meet me. I meet my friend Alex and his girlfriend, and then Kimberly comes walking up. She looks gorgeous, and my feelings for her shift to one of genuine affection. We have a kick-ass night and kiss for hours in the club until it is time to leave. Nothing sexual, at least we are back on, it seems.

A few days later, we go out again; she calls me and asks, "So are we going to make it official and see what happens? I'm not interested in just being there for an occasional booty call." I say yes, and we meet up at the original Outback Steakhouse for lunch. Throughout our meal, Kimberly expresses her feelings and needs while I intently listen. Everything she is saying is what I would like to experience together with her. We are a thing, a forever kind of love, and I love everything about Kimberly, *Zen Soma*.

39

Pot Life

Halloween's eve, and we subsequently hear the news that we are signing our deferral papers next week in New York. When I look at my parenting schedule, I notice that the trip to New York will be when I have my boys. I will need someone to watch them. I try to think of who I can ask, but all my friends are away. I try to call my old TKE fraternity brother Dennis, but he is a cop now and refuses to answer my phone calls. I finally get through to his wife Dena and beg her to help me.

I call and pathetically beg to say, "Dena, can you please watch my kids so I can get this crap resolved, please?"

Dena responds, "You know we can't do that, Kevin, right? Because of Dennis's job. What if someone is watching us? He could lose his job and his pension with it. It's too risky." I am so upset I cannot hold back. I yell and call Dena some names I am not proud of and hang up on her. A new low for me, a place I feel alone, no friends. You find out who your friends are when something like this happens.

Since I am dating Kimberly now, I hesitantly request her

help. I couldn't tell her the real reason I was going to New York, so I make up some story about an old fraternity brother's father dying. She agrees to help and saves my ass; I regret I lied about it. She deserves better.

We fly to New York dressed in a suit and meet up at the federal court building coffee shop. We all have a quick bite to eat and walk inside. As we approach the chamber, some signs read keep quiet, no cell phones. We quietly make our way up toward the front and sit in a hard wooden chair. I am running everything through my head, all that we have gone through—the crazy adventure. Lessons learned. After an hour of waiting, the judge opens his door and marches into the soundless courtroom. We rise to our feet, and then we sit again.

He sits and reads from a statement and asks us if we will agree to this and says, "You realize if you do not comply….?" We all quickly and loudly say yes, Sir, one at a time, and then we conclude. Once we get out in front of the courthouse, we snap a picture on the steps as free men.

We all sigh a deep sigh of relief, and Justin yells out, "Let's go to the bar!" We all agree, and Billy's Lawyer Tim says in his New Orleans accent, "I know a place right around the corner. Let's go, boys!" I call my old Oneonta roommate Homey, and he meets us at the bar as we celebrate. I am hugging everyone, and then I hug Homey as he walks in.

"Congratulations, bro. It must be a good day for you."

I sigh and say, "oh, you do not understand. It is the worst year of my life. We're so lucky we got off."

He reluctantly gets up and gives me another hug, and says, "Alright, man, I got to go. Breanne needs me to pick up some shit from her office on my way home."

We say goodbye and then I go over to the group, and I sit next to Tim and ask, "So do you think we can get our cars and all that cash they seized now? Now that we are not guilty anymore?"

He looks at me and says, "Nah, that's all gone."

"Really?" I ask, "You don't think there's a chance since all the charges dropped?"

He shakes his head and smiles, and says, "They're gone. No chance."

"Damn," I say. "That sucks!"

Tim puts his arm around me and says, "Now C'mon, man. You guys just got all your shit dropped. You're a free man! You're all free! When it's all said and done, you get to go home to your wife and kids tonight. What's that worth to you?"

I agree and ask, "So what about Stan and Johnny, Lou, and Louisiana? Any word on their case?"

"I can't comment on that case, but I will say it looks a little more likely not to end up celebrating like us here today," Tim says.

Justin proceeds up to us and says, "Tim, I know we paid you a flat fee, but since the case concluded, do we get any of that money back now? We sure could use it!"

I cringe and know what his response is going to be. He chuckles a bit and says, "No, man, that's not how it works."

I knew he was going to say that. All our seized stuff, gone, but we are ultimately free.

As time goes by, we lose track of Stan and all the other guys we once worked with. When things are going wrong and under government surveillance, you get paranoid about everything and everyone. No one wants to talk to anyone amid fears of further legal troubles.

* * *

A year passes before I am googling Stan to see what had happened to him and see the report about their attorney Don, *Peculiar Wares*, *Geno-trition*. It turns out attorney Jim D. was right. There is no letter from Louisiana's Attorney General, Buddy Caldwell, allowing their products' sale. Their attorney Don had never even met Buddy Caldwell, let alone get a letter from him.

They all took their chances and went to trial, and it didn't work out well for them. They were all found guilty of conspiring to distribute synthetic drugs, conspiring to introduce misbranded drugs into interstate commerce, and money laundering. Their trial lasted eight days with thirty plus witnesses, and it takes the jury only six hours to find them guilty.

The judge shows no mercy at sentencing. Lou and Johnny each receive one hundred seventeen months, Lloyd seventy months, Jay sixty-one months, and Stan got forty-two months. They must pay nearly a million dollars in fines. Attorney Don receives one hundred twenty months in prison sentencing. They also order him to serve six more years of supervised release with permanent disbarring.

Back in Tampa and officially released from our pretrial services nightmare, we can smoke weed again. All of us show up at the pre-trial officer Nathan's office in downtown Tampa and ride up the elevator to the pretrial services floor. We are all sure it will be our last visit, but we are about to find out. All of us are nervous and excited that our monitoring is concluding.

Nathan walks over and greets us, "Come on in, guys. There are just a few things I need you guys to sign, and that will be it." He hands us all a bunch of papers and goes over them. We quickly sign each page one by one.

He takes all our signed forms and says, "So with these forms completed, there's nothing else I need from you today. Questions?"

I ask, "Will you ever need anything else from us again?"

Justin laughs, "Yeah, do we ever have to come back?"

Nathan jokingly questions, "Do you want to come back?"

Billy stands up and says," No, we don't."

With the same straight face, he always has, Nathan says," Alright, then I guess we're done."

I question," For good?"

Nathan replies, "For good. Unless you find yourself back here on additional charges."

We all shout and declare, "No, no, no."

We all shake his hand, thank him, and bolt out the door.

Billy immediately calls worker Justin and says, "You have it?" Billy's eyes look at me as if to say he's got it.

"He's got it," Billy smiles and says.

Justin and I ruptured into laughter and applauded high five. Billy laughs. Then we all roar in relief. We practically fly in the car back to Ybor. We pull in and meet Justin, Nate, and Nate's brother Ben and his girlfriend Michelle up above the La France Boutique, Nate's Mom's building. They present us with wax-dabs, a bunch of fresh buds pre-packed in a glass bowl, and a stack of pre-rolled joints. Our eyes are wide with disbelief.

"Enjoy, dudes." Nate says with a red-eye stoned-out laugh, "Enjoy."

I state," I want a massive dab right now."

Nate answers, "I got the torch right here, brotha," and he

fires it up. I lean into a brand-new custom signature Illadelph glass smoking piece already set up for us and take a deep ass draw of smoke. I cough so hard I nearly spit up blood. Within seconds I am beyond stoned, and I love it! Mary, is that you? Hello, is it me you're looking for?

Anyone that smokes pot knows just what that moment would be like for them. Please understand that I love marijuana. We all enjoy and love it. When you get that taken away from you for so long, that first step back into the pot life is sweeter than ever. I grab a few buds and some joints and shove them in my pockets. I was as content as I've ever been.

It feels like freedom, but we weren't entirely free until we finally smoked again. We inhale a little deeper; it tastes yummier, and the high is a little more potent than any other time in our life, and we all know it. We laugh and hug each other like we just won the battle, and we had.

Back at my house in my special place outside next to the swimming pool, I sit and smoke—a free man. My son's faces come to the forefront of my mind as I shake my head back and forth softly in disbelief. I dodged a bullet with this one, I consider.

I close my eyes, and my face tilts upright. The warm sun touches my eyes and cascades over my face and neck. Ahhhhhh. Breathing the warmth of freedom, I recall my younger years at *the OBI*, college, friends along the way, even friendships that fell on the wayside. Back then, I wanted to be cool, and I wanted to feel accepted. I just wanted a tribe, a group of people who enjoyed the same things, such as music and cannabis culture.

Hot Wax is that tribe for me, my community. I made some mistakes along the way and came out wiser. I used to think pot life was like getting your deepest desire only to have it taken away. Still, I realize pot life is about embracing who I am and understanding my family and tribe are my real heart's desire. I enjoy having fun, and it is time to do that and leave a legacy behind.

The end... or the beginning?

www.ingramcontent.com/pod-product-compliance
Lightning Source LLC
Chambersburg PA
CBHW060318030426
42336CB00011B/1101